EDITOR: MARTIN WINDROW

OSPREY MILITARY · **MEN-AT-ARMS SERIES** · **39**

THE BRITISH ARMY IN NORTH AMERICA 1775-1783

Text by
ROBIN MAY
Colour plates by
G A EMBLETON

D1414971

First published in Great Britain in 1974 by
Osprey, a division of Reed Consumer Books Ltd.
Michelin House, 81 Fulham Road,
London SW3 6RB
and Auckland, Melbourne, Singapore and Toronto

ISBN 0 85045 195 7

The wide selection of books about the American
Revolution contains few written from the point of
view of the British Army. One that the author has
found particularly helpful is *The British Army in the
American Revolution* by Edward E. Curtis (New
Haven and London, 1926; EP Publishing, 1972).
A fruitful source book for quotations has been
The Spirit of Seventy-Six edited by Henry Steele
Commager and Richard B. Morris (New York,
1958/1967), and some of the points made in
Reginald Hargreaves's *The Bloodybacks* (London,
1968) have been most instructive. In addition Sir
John Fortescue's monumental *History of the British
Army*, Vol. 3 (London, 1902) is always valuable.

Filmset in Great Britain
Printed through World Print Ltd, Hong Kong

Introduction

The British have rarely disliked a war more than the American Revolution and have never been less eager to serve in the armed forces of the crown. If it had not been for Scotsmen, who joined the army in considerable numbers, recruiting would have been an even bigger fiasco than it was.

The Whig Opposition was against the war to the extent of sometimes glorying publicly in British defeats, and, as history was mostly written by Whig historians in the following century, the notable achievements of the redcoats in America were played down. When battle honours were distributed, none at all were awarded for the Revolution, a shameful omission, yet the marvel is not that the troops fought so badly, but so well. At American textbook level, the redcoats have been made into ogres, though to balance this many of the more sympathetic comments on them have been written by Americans.

Courage was never in short supply. For sheer guts, the redcoats' behaviour at Bunker Hill, Saratoga and other bloody encounters has rarely been excelled. The fact that some commanders refused to serve against the Americans hardly helped to achieve victory, while others, including Howe and Clinton, only crossed the Atlantic out of loyalty to the King. So did Burgoyne, though, unlike the other two, he had no sympathy with the Americans, and later called them a 'rabble in arms'. He simply did not want to serve in America, though in the event he was ambitious enough. Much may be forgiven 'Gentleman Johnny', however, for he was 'the soldiers' friend' and was loved by them.

Howe – 'Good-natured Billy Howe' – is widely regarded as a sluggard who continually let slip chances of finishing off the war in 1776. In fact, though no military genius and a lover of a quiet

life, we can now, thanks to American historians, see him holding out an olive branch to his enemies, never hitting them too hard, but hoping to encourage them to make peace. And, as we shall see, he was also continually short of supplies which mostly had to be shipped across the Atlantic, a fact buried under stories of living off the land, plunder and rape.

The difficulties of campaigning in America and gross inefficiency and corruption at home were

Lieutenant-General John Burgoyne – 'Gentleman Johnny' – playwright, politician and 'the soldiers' friend'.

far more deadly enemies of the redcoats than the generals' conduct, blundering as it sometimes was.

The Americans won, but only just, and then thanks to foreign intervention and a small number of patriots dedicated, valiant and continually let down by their own people. Washington and a hard core of always loyal, always dependable regiments stand in magnificent contrast to a mean, bickering Congress, and part-time soldiers almost coming and going as they pleased. The standard generalization about the American Revolution

Sir Henry Clinton, Howe's successor as Commander-in-Chief in America.

was first made by John Adams, the second President, who claimed that a third of his countrymen wanted a revolution, a third were against it and a third were neutral. If that was so only a small proportion of the Rebels were prepared to be militant in the true sense of the word.

As for George Washington, lost as he sometimes seems under a mountain of legend, because he was so let down by his countrymen and because he was no great general, his achievement was all the more extraordinary. This complex man, to whom duty and patriotism were not mere words, deserves more from his compatriots than a halo.

He was a giant, and Britons can be proud that he, too, was British.

The redcoat, having won victory after victory except when victory most mattered, finally left for home in November 1783, his humour undimmed. The very last man to go, having lowered the Union flag on Staten Island and cut the halliards, proceeded to grease the staff. As they rowed away, they were able to enjoy the sight of their late enemies trying to raise the Stars and Stripes and not succeeding until cleats had been hammered up the pole and the flag nailed into place.

Some redcoats may have also chuckled a little at the final peace treaty, for though Britain lost her American Colonies, she did not come out of the war so badly considering that she had France, Spain and Holland against her as well by the end of it. True, the glorious days of the Year of Miracles, 1759, were no more and the prestige of Britain, so high in 1763, had slumped badly. But Rodney's victory over de Grasse in 1782 had saved the West Indies, Gibraltar had not fallen, France was almost bankrupt, Spain had problems at home and in North America, and, though it was not realized at the time, the Loyalists who settled in Canada were a magnificent investment for the future. In the immediate future, they and the redcoats were to help throw the Americans out of Canada in the War of 1812.

*   *   *

The book which follows is not an account of the war and its strategy, but offers a short examination of the organization of the British Army in America and Britain at the time of the Revolution, with particular emphasis on the redcoat and his war.

Raising an Army

When the Seven Years War ended in 1763, Great Britain proceeded to decimate the army which had done so much to win her an empire. All infantry of the line were disbanded above the 70th Foot and all cavalry above the 18th Light Dragoons. The establishment was therefore a miserable 17,500, 3,000 of whom were the emergency force so aptly known as the 'Corps of

A private of the Picket Company of the 11th Foot, in about 1771. These companies were the forerunners of the regimental light companies which appeared very shortly afterwards. The cap appears to be fur-trimmed; the crown, royal cipher and regimental number are in brass. The red coat of the 11th was lined white and faced dark green, with red and green stripes in the regimental lace. (Reproduced by gracious permission of H.M. The Queen)

A private of the Picket Company of the 13th Foot, in that regiment's yellow-faced coat; again, the cap ornament is brass. (Reproduced by gracious permission of H.M. The Queen)

Invalids'. There were also 1,800 gunners and sappers, and 12,000 men were on the Irish establishment.

The Colonies were allowed 10,000 men, excluding 4,000 for Minorca and Gibraltar, and, though the East India Company had its own forces, this meant that the rest of the Empire was pitifully under-policed. Hatred of standing armies at home and abroad could hardly be taken further.

The events leading up to the American Revolution are not the concern of this book, but several points must be stressed where the redcoats were concerned. Firstly, though many Britons were not convinced that Canada was worth possessing, none doubted the importance of the American Colonies and the sugar-rich West Indies. The government's methods in this period were blundering in the extreme. True, Britain had spent a fortune to win Canada from the French and make the thirteen American Colonies safe, so therefore felt obliged to extract money from Americans to help pay the cost of keeping troops in America, and also to ease the National Debt. But to use sledge-hammer tactics instead of tact to get the money from independent-minded Americans was fatuous. Yet only the most far-sighted could foresee an actual war breaking out between the mother country and her own people in America so soon after the bells had been ringing for the destruction of New France.

But the government, even if it could not foresee a revolution, should have realized the folly of cutting down the army because of what happened the very year the war ended. Pontiac's dramatic rebellion, the last real chance the Indians ever had of driving the whites back to the Atlantic, should have made ministers at once aware of the folly of cuts as the better of two white evils, not least because Pontiac was pro-French. Perhaps because, after sensational successes elsewhere, his main campaign against Detroit just failed, the lessons of his rebellion were not grasped.

So when the Revolution started in 1775, the British Army was only 48,647 strong, with 39,294 infantry, 6,869 cavalry and 2,484 artillery. The breakdown below of their locations comes to slightly fewer because it leaves out the artillery, plus twenty independent companies of invalids on garrison duty, though it does include the 41st, a regiment of invalids.

General Sir Guy Carleton, saviour of Canada and later, as Lord Dorchester, her first Governor-General.

LOCATION OF THE ARMY IN 1775

	Infantry	Effectives	Cavalry	Effectives
England	19 regts	11,396	16 regts	4,151
Scotland	1 regt	474		
Isle of Man	3 comps	142		
Ireland	21 regts	9,815	12 regts	2,718
Minorca	5 regts	2,385		
Gibraltar	7 regts	3,339		
West Indies	3 regts	1,909		
America	18 regts	8,580		
Africa	1 corps	214		
	Total	38,254	Total	6,869

This makes a grand total of 45,123 men to guard an empire, plus gunners, some invalids, and the soldiers of the East India Company, together with a Royal Navy at almost the lowest ebb in its history under the Earl of Sandwich, who was 'Too infamous to have a friend, Too bad for bad men to commend.'

Six years after this, by which time the military war was over in America except for skirmishes and the formalities, the army had reached the 110,000 mark, 57,000 of them stationed in America and the West Indies. This does not include the seventy or so Loyalist regiments and formations, the 30,000 German mercenaries and the fluctuating number of Indians who fought on the British side.

Recruiting has never been more difficult than for this war. Apart from the unpopularity of the conflict, the 1770s were the last years before the Industrial Revolution introduced a large number of the working classes to a fate worse than taking

the King's shilling – the nightmare world of prison-like factories. They were the last years when Britain was more an agricultural than an industrial nation, when even the poorest countrymen could expect to eat well, when enclosures had not yet wrecked the rural way of life.

So the temptation to join up was minimal for poor pay, savage discipline and bad food, combined with the prospect of fighting fellow Britons, was enough to put off all but born fighters and adventurers. Fortunately, Scotland at least was full of both.

The pay of a private soldier was eightpence a day, but most of it was promptly taken away from him. Sixpence allegedly went for subsistence, though some of the precious pennies were put aside to pay for clothing, medicine and the repair of arms. Much of the remaining twopence was deducted to pay the Paymaster-General, the Chelsea Hospital a recruit was so unlikely to

Ein Britischer Soldat auf dem Posten, in der Canadischen Winter Kleidung. 1766.

A British soldier stationed in Canada in 1778 – not, as the picture's caption suggests, 1766. (All Friedrich von Germann's other drawings in this series bear the later date.) He wears a white blanket coat, or capote, with a hood; it has light blue trim at cuff and hem, a light blue rosette on the hip, and is fastened with tapes of the same colour. Long blue overalls, or gaiter trousers, are worn, and an underjacket with sleeves of strong white corduroy would have been typical. The red-skulled cap has brown fur trim and tail. (New York Public Library)

Aerial view of Fort Niagara, which could hardly be less like the log stockade of Hollywood legend. Its stirring history stretches from 1679 to 1815, when it was handed back to the U.S.A. – it had been taken from the French in 1759. The redoubts date from 1770–1, while the stone blockhouses, each mounting two cannon on the gun-deck, have walls five feet thick. In the foreground are the gate and the south blockhouse; on the right is the north block-house; in the far background is the 'castle' with its bakehouse; isolated on the left is the magazine; and to the left of the blockhouse in the foreground is a range of store buildings. (Old Fort Niagara Association Incorporated)

Fort Niagara – the south blockhouse is shown – was not only very strongly built but was strategically important. During the Revolution it was the main base for Loyalist and Indian guerillas, notably Butler's Rangers and the Iroquois led by Joseph Brant. (Old Fort Niagara Association Incorporated and Grove McClellan)

Engraved powder horn of unusual interest, inscribed with a detailed map and the legend: PER ROBERTSON / CORPLL IN CAPT PEYTONS COMP:Y / IN THE 9TH REGT / 1ST AUGUSTINE / MARCH 11 1767, and: THE CITY OF HAVANNA ILLUMINATED AT THE EMBARKATION OF THE BRITISH [sic] TROOPS JULY THE 7TH 1763 (Metropolitan Museum of Art)

reach, the regimental agent, etc. The system of pay and stoppages was unbelievably complicated, but the result was the same – the soldier got next to nothing.

Barracks were few in Britain in the 1770s, so the recruit was likely to be under canvas, or, more probably, in lodgings where his presence was greatly resented. Discipline was eighteenth-century traditional, the only difference from earlier times being that the lash was the universal penalty for most crimes. Other tortures like the 'horse' and 'running the gauntlet' were not being phased out for humanitarian reasons, but simply because flogging was simpler, 1,000 or more lashes still being a frequent sentence.

Food was generally appalling, and continued to be so when the soldier reached America. Legend has it that the redcoats lived comfortably off the land, and legend is wrong, as we shall see in the next chapter. Recruits in Britain were often so underfed in their dingy billets that they were scarcely able to endure the drill that turned them into remarkably good soldiers.

Most of the major battles of the Revolution were fought on European patterns, so the red coats of the men were not in themselves a menace to safety, even though the Americans from the start picked off their officers. As the war progressed dress regulations were relaxed, making it easier for the soldier to fight. The stock was not yet a tortuous high leather collar, but was more often made of velvet or horsehair, and gaiters had been black since 1768. But it still took the average soldier up to three hours to get himself ready for a parade, on which a slight movement or a badly

arranged head of hair – unhygienic grease and powder were the rule – could get him 100 lashes or more.

As for equipment, it might weigh as much as sixty pounds, though some have claimed – probably wrongly – that it sometimes weighed almost twice as much. Burgoyne considered sixty pounds too much, and the following revealing report about equipment, dated 15 June 1784, soon after the war was over, shows that notice was taken of complaints if senior officers made them. It is a Report of the Proceedings of a Committee of General Officers Regarding the Equipment of Soldiers, and the listed recommendations received approval:

1 Ordnance Cartridge Box at present in use found to be inconvenient.
2 Powder-Horns and Bullet-Bags of Light Infantry were never used during the late war.
3 Matches & Match-Cases of Grenadiers are becoming obsolete.
4 Grenadiers' swords were never used during the last war. [It was proposed that all these articles be abandoned.]
5 The whole battalion to be accoutred alike, with the addition of two articles for the Light Infantry, e.g., Hatchet & Priming Horn, which may be carried either with the knapsack or as the Commanding Officer shall think most convenient.
6 Shoulder-belts to be of equal breadth, and to have the Ammunition divided; to carry the Pouch on the right side, and the Magazine on the left.

Inside of a reconstruction of a late 18th-century British Army knapsack. The light tan blanket, with two brown stripes woven in one side, and a broad arrow and royal cipher stamp, is copied from an original from H.M.S. *Jersey*, of 1783 vintage, now in the New Windsor, N.Y., Cantonment Collection. (P. R. N. Katcher Collection)

7 Pouch & Bayonet-Belts to be of Buff Leather & both to be 2 inches broad, the Bayonet-Carriage [frog] to slip on & off the belt with two loops.
8 A Leather cap worn by some of the Light Infantry during the late war is strongly recommended.
9 Propose a black woollen cloth gaiter with white metal buttons & without stiff tops in place of the black linen gaiters at present in use.

A Royal Artillery cartridge pouch; the large pouch conceals a wooden block drilled for nine cartridges. The frog at the front of the belt held fast the cord of a priming flask and may have held vent prickers. (Charleston Museum)

The badge on the Royal Artillery pouch illustrated above is made of brass and backed with red leather. (Charleston Museum)

So something had been learnt from the campaign in America. Back in 1775, it must have seemed to some that there would be no campaigns from which to learn, for recruiting was practically stationary. In December, Edward Harvey, the Adjutant-General, lamented: 'Sad work everywhere in recruiting. In these damned times we must exert zeal.'

He was right, for apart from the reasons for not joining the army already noted there were other disadvantages. Service was normally for life and postings abroad could go on for decades. Notoriously, the 38th Foot was trapped in the West Indies for sixty years! And the deep unpopularity of soldiers was as rampant as at any time in the century. At least the sailor, pressed, flogged and wretched, could – and often did, even at this dismal time in naval history – comfort himself with the thought that he was the nation's pride.

Volunteers joined up for three years or the duration, but, except for in Scotland, there were pitifully few of them in 1775–6. Some recruiting parties in their despair levied invalids and pensioners, and even Roman Catholics, unwelcome before 1775, were recruited.

Less successful was an attempt to enlist 20,000 Russian mercenaries, or to entice a Scotch brigade back from service with the Dutch. This led to the hiring of Germans from Hesse-Cassel and elsewhere. However, the Highlands proved good ground for recruiting parties, many clansmen coming forward to get away from grim conditions at home, or to seek glory, or both. Lowlanders also came forward, some even refusing bounty, and the families of these who went from certain towns were supported by those who stayed behind. The English, Irish and Welsh showed no such ardour.

Up until 1778, volunteers received one and a half guineas, but as there were far too few of them, pardoned criminals and deserters were welcomed. Five feet six and a half inches was the required height, though youngsters who looked as if they might grow were enlisted, whereas the lame, the ruptured and those prone to fits were not.

British infantry officer's sword, now in the City of Lancaster Museum, of the type commonly carried just before and during the Revolution. A crimson and gold sword-knot was usually attached to the guard. (Peter W. Joslin)

After 1778, when Saratoga brought the French in, recruiting became more urgent. Volunteers got three pounds and, as in 1775, a discharge in three years or at the end of the war; and, in Scotland and the London area, the 'able-bodied idle and disorderly' were pressed for at least five years or until the end of hostilities. The age limits were seventeen to forty-five. The 'idle' persons elsewhere in Britain were left to work the land.

This scheme, too, failed, so in 1779 volunteers got three and a half guineas and the right to set up in business after service wherever they chose, whatever local corporations might say. The wounded were to get similar privileges. The pressed men, meanwhile, could now be as short as five feet four inches and as old as fifty. New sorts of rogues could be taken, and the whole country could be scoured for them. The only escape was to join the militia, a fair ploy as Britain seemed to be in danger of invasion.

Despite desertions, self-maimings and fights with the press-gangs, just enough men were found

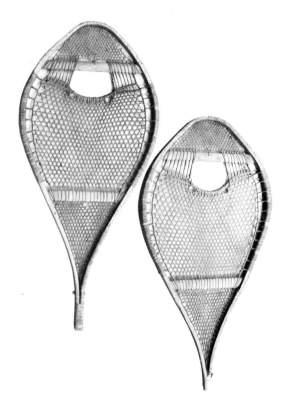

Snowshoes, dating from _c._ 1780 – the essential requirement for all troops in the North American winter. (Courtesy, City of Liverpool Museums)

– 1,463 in south Britain between March and October 1779 – but what saved the army was the fact that many now came forward to volunteer to avoid being pressed and to benefit by the very fair terms.

In 1778, twelve new regiments of foot were raised and seventeen more had been raised by 1780. Four regiments of light dragoons were raised between 1778 and 1781. Old regiments were enlarged, a system the King preferred as he suspected (rightly in many cases) that colonels of the new regiments would place too many relatives in them. Towns, too, raised regiments – the 80th (Royal Edinburgh Volunteers) was one – and also gave generous bounties. Less happily, the system of drafting was much in evidence, a badly mauled regiment being forced to send its officers, N.C.O.s and drummers home to recruit while its surviving privates transferred to another regiment also in need of men, but not destitute. This seriously interfered with _esprit de corps_. Some draftees of the Black Watch mutinied rather than join the 83rd and be forced to abandon their kilts, and thirty were killed in a pitched battle.

The recruit to the infantry found himself in a regiment of some 477 men divided into ten companies forming a single battalion. One company consisted of grenadiers, who no longer hurled grenades, but were the tallest and strongest men in the regiment. Another was made up of light infantrymen, wiry troops who were the regiment's crack shots. These picked men were placed on the flanks.

The recruit was subjected to endless arms drill, often a rugged ordeal on inadequate rations. The basic infantry weapon was the 'Brown Bess' musket, with a carbine for the cavalry, while fusiliers carried a fusil. The finest British firearm of the war, the Ferguson breech-loader invented by the dashing Major Patrick Ferguson, was only used by 100 or so picked marksmen in America.

[Regimental doctors, as recruits found, varied from good to ghastly]. And as for the consolations of religion, it was an irreligious age, and though each regiment officially had a chaplain, few ever appeared. Sergeant Lamb, the diarist and surgeon's mate of the 9th, claimed he knew many pious soldiers, and there was no reason for him to lie. Despite the origins of many men, and the

The burial of General Frazer at Saratoga, 1777: an engraving by W. Nutter after J. Graham, published in 1794. Although stylized, the costumes of the figures in this painting are correct in their details of campaign dress in North America. Kneeling and kissing Frazer's hand is his nephew, who served in a battalion formed from regimental light companies. He wears a very short jacket (waistcoat?) and Indian leggings. Other figures wear short jackets and long overalls. (National Army Museum)

brutish lives they had endured, the average redcoat cannot have been so very different from his successors a century or more later. William Cobbett, the great radical politician and writer, thought highly of soldiers. He joined the army in 1784 and became a sergeant-major. He once wrote: 'I like soldiers, as a class in life, better than any other description of men. Their conversation is more pleasing to me; they have generally seen more than other men; they have less vulgar prejudice about them. Amongst soldiers, less than amongst any other description of men, have I observed the vices of lying and hypocrisy.'

Written permission was needed from an officer for Cobbett's admired private soldiers to marry. The regulations for wives and women on campaign belong to the next chapter. In barracks at home – though true barracks only date from the 1790s – husbands and wives were entitled to screened-off beds in barrack-rooms.

As for the standard of officers, it was perhaps higher than it had been in the Seven Years War, in which so many of them had previously fought. This is not the book to argue the few pros and many cons of the purchase system of commissions which held so many officers without private means to junior ranks and allowed mere youths to command them. There was no general in the Revolution quite so ineffective as Abercromby of Fort Ticonderoga (1758), but nor was there a Wolfe. And Sir William Howe, regardless of his feelings about the war, was not the equal of his incomparable elder brother, Lord George Augustus Howe, killed at Ticonderoga just before

Thomas Boothby Parkyns, 15th Light Dragoons, 1776–81. Although the 15th Dragoons did not serve in America, the dashing style of helmet, the cut of the uniform and the horse furniture are typical of the period and of this class of troops. (National Army Museum)

who could, plenty of career officers who got on with the job, along with a hard core of fine N.C.O.s. And under them was that much-abused, sorely tried, usually valiant and humorous man of war, the redcoat.

RECRUITING
Two contrasting methods

Major Boyle Roche in action in Ireland in August, 1775, as reported by the *Dublin Journal*. First he organized a procession:

Major Roche, bearing a large Purse of Gold,
Captain Cowley
A great number of likely recruits
An elegant Band of Music, consisting of French Horns, Hautboys, Clarionets, and Bassoons, playing 'God Save the King'
A large Brewers Dray with five Barrels of Beer, the Horse richly caparisoned and ornamented with ribbons,
Two Draymen with Cockades, to serve the Beer,
The Recruiting Serjeant,
Drums and Fifes,
Another Division of Recruits,
The Recruiting Soldiers,
A prodigious concourse of Spectators.

The following speech was then made by Major Roche to the Populace.

'Gentlemen and Fellow Countrymen–
'Being appointed, through the Favour of our most excellent Governor, to raise a Body of Men for the Service of his Majesty, I think it the most happy Circumstance of my Life to be the Instrument of leading you forth to Honour and Renown.
'The Laurels fought for and obtained in all Parts of the Globe last War, have procured us a Fame so glorious as not to be equalled by any People in any Age – a Fame not to be sullied by the Assaults of Prejudice nor the Effects of Time. Not an Action in which we were not victorious, not a Siege in which we were not honoured. Will you, my dear Countrymen, permit those Laurels to fade or those Actions to be forgotten? No, forbid it Heaven. Let us now that we have it in our Power, convey to latest Posterity a Renewal of our Fidelity, and a Confirmation of our Loyalty. A more critical Period never presented itself, nor had we ever a fairer Opportunity of shewing our Attachment to the illustrious House

Abercromby did his worst, which included allowing the Black Watch to be massacred. Ironically, Howe, Burgoyne and Clinton were all Members of Parliament and it was not considered wrong for a general-politician to return to London in the winter and speak in the House.

One often fortunate factor at this time was that no officer was forced to serve overseas. This not only meant that lunatics and infants were not obliged to take the field, but that the ambitious might rise faster because many officers preferred to stay at home on half pay rather than serve. To reach the top in the 1770s it was best to be in the Guards or the cavalry, but that was to hold good for many years to come.

The real stumbling-block was the number of serving soldiers who simply did not wish to fight Americans. Lord Percy, later Duke of Northumberland, whose conduct on the first day of the Revolution helped save the retreating British Army, was one of many officers who could not stomach the war. After distinguished service in 1776, he returned home.

Fortunately for British arms, there were plenty

Barrels of beer and grandiose speeches might suit the Irish, but not the Black Watch, whose 2nd Battalion was raised again in 1779 after having been disbanded for some years. Stern Highlanders expected, and got, stern recruiting posters. Here is an excerpt clearly aimed at men of iron: 'You who, uncorrupted by the universal depravity of your southern countrymen, have withstood, unmoveable as a rock, all the assaults of Surrounding Luxury and Depravity. You who, while others, effeminated by voluptuous refinements, and irrecoverably lost to honour, lolling in the arms of Pleasure, can see the danger of their country with a criminal indifference . . .' etc.

THE PRICES OF COMMISSIONS IN 1776

Listed below are the most expensive commissions and the least expensive, those omitted being those for the Dragoon Guards and Dragoons, and the Foot Guards. Artillery commissions were not purchased. When it is realized that an infantry

The regulation bearskin cap of the period. The plate is white metal, five inches high, with the background japanned black to make the motif stand out. The cap is twelve inches high without the fur. Sometimes the backs were ornamented with cords and tassels. The plate was more or less the same design for both drummers and grenadiers; the drummers' being embellished with drums and trophies of flags. (National Army Museum)

of Hanover, than the present, as his Majesty's deluded subjects in America are in open Rebellion, and, like unnatural children, would destroy their ever indulgent Parent, forgetting the Torrents of Blood spilt, and Heaps of Treasure extended for their Preservation.

'His Sacred Majesty now calls us, and our Fidelity obliges us, and I hope your Inclination prompts you, to obey the dictates of so good and lenient a Master. Let us then, my brave and loyal countrymen, join Hearts and Hands, and cheerfully step forth in the glorious Cause of our Creator, our King, and our Country. We have it in our Power by Unanimity and inexhaustible Resources, to reduce those daring Rebels to a due Obedience to their Sovereign, and Submission to the Laws of their Country, which will give a fresh conviction to all Europe that Hibernian Laurels have not faded by Time, but on the contrary are increasing in Bloom and Verdure.'

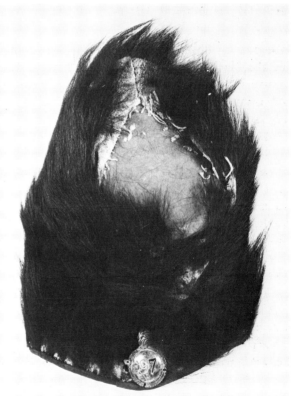

Back view of a grenadier's cap of the 97th Foot, 1794-6. On the back was an oval red patch usually bearing the regimental number, and badge if any. (National Army Museum)

13

major got a mere seventeen shillings a day less heavy stoppages, and how much it cost him to buy his commission, it can be seen how important private means were. The whole purchase system was a highly organized and profitable business, the key figure being the colonel of a regiment who, having bought or obtained his command, could do what he liked with it, recouping his expenses by selling commissions, and using his annual allotment of funds to the benefit of his men or to line his own pockets. The nation accepted the purchase system, not just because it was a corrupt age, but because it was felt that well-heeled officers would have a stake in the *status quo* and not be a menace to the state.

FIRST AND SECOND TROOPS OF HORSE-GUARDS

Commissions	Prices
First Lieutenant-Colonel	£5,500
Second Lieutenant-Colonel	£5,100
Cornet and Major	£4,300
Guidon and Major	£4,100
Exempt and Captain	£2,700
Brigadier and Lieutenant or Adjutant and Lieutenant	£1,500
Sub-Brigadier and Cornet	£1,200

MARCHING REGIMENTS OF FOOT

Commissions	Prices
Lieutenant-Colonel	£3,500
Major	£2,600
Captain	£1,500
Captain-Lieutenant	£800
Lieutenant	£500
Ensign	£400

Coat of the 101st Foot, 1781–5. This valuable and all-too-rare relic of 18th-century military dress displays the cut of a typical coat of the day, and the crowned regimental number on the buttons. Note the pockets in the tails, and the unusual button layout on the cuffs. (National Army Museum)

The Redcoats' War

When the 'shot heard round the world' rang out on Lexington Green on 19 April 1775 some redcoats at least must have sighed with relief. For most of the previous seven or so years, life in Boston for unwelcome British troops had been not unlike their successors' life in Ulster in the 1970s, though even more unpleasant.

The food in the 1770s was worse, billets were worse and restrictions on any sort of action were worse, to say nothing of harsher discipline and distance from home. The classic confrontation, the so-called 'Boston Massacre' of 1770, found nine men of the 29th driven beyond endurance to shoot at a murderous mob, whose victims were promptly canonized. The soldiers were saved from being convicted of murder on the most tainted evidence by the honourable lawyer, John Adams, cousin of the revolutionary propagandist and hatemonger, Sam Adams. The one officer involved and six of his men were found innocent, two others were branded on their thumbs for manslaughter.

There was no reason for Bostonians, or, indeed, any Americans to love the redcoats, even though they were the soldiers who had freed them from the French menace, but it was hard that they should become the whipping-boys for their country's mistakes. After Lexington the redcoat found himself transformed by the New England propaganda machine into a monster, the machine seeing to it that stories of rape, arson and murder reached England before the official account. Lucky the country to suffer invasion from such mild monsters!

The flood of troops needed to fight in America, once the scope of the war was realized after Bunker (Breed's) Hill, created a major transport problem. Cork was then the main embarkation port for North America, and ships used as transports varied from fine East Indiamen to old and unseaworthy hulks. They were sent across the Atlantic in convoys of up to twelve ships, sometimes even more, and there was an endless flow of victuallers as well.

Officers seem to have made real efforts to keep their men happy on the transports, but it was uphill work. The situation was candidly summed up by a Guards officer on his way to join Howe in New York, who wrote, 'There was continued destruction in the foretops, the pox above-board, the plague between decks, hell in the forecastle, the devil at the helm.'

The loss of horses could be terrible if a voyage went on longer than expected, and their destruction undoubtedly affected the results of certain battles. Howe could have turned his victory at Brandywine in 1777 into a total rout if he had commanded a well-mounted corps of light cavalry, and as for Clinton, on his expedition from New York to Charleston in 1779–80, he lost every single horse.

Sailors were in short supply to man the transports and victuallers, and there was usually a shortage of ships, too, made worse because the authorities in America failed to turn the transports round and send them home quickly enough. Add bribery, corruption, gross inefficiency in many quarters and inter-departmental quarrelling, and it is hardly surprising that the redcoats were usually short of food and equipment.

The transport situation in America was less bad than in the French and Indian War when Braddock and other British commanders sometimes despaired of getting hold of wagons. These were usually hired in the Revolution, everything from four-horse wagons to sledges. Special vehicles were used as ammunition carts, others as hospital wagons and forge carts 'compleat with anvils and

Another expedient adopted before the official sanction for a light company in each regiment was the 'Highland Company' – this plate illustrates a private of the Highland Company of the 25th Foot, a Lowland Scottish regiment. The men of this company evidently had their coats cropped to the length worn by Highland regiments. The uniform is scarlet faced yellow, with red and blue stripes in the lace. The cap is of black fur with a red front flap worked with a white device. (Reproduced by gracious permission of H.M. The Queen)

bellows'. Horses, too, were bought or captured. The drivers of the vehicles were hired civilians. A single statistic will show the scope of the problem: from December 1776 to March 1780, Howe and Clinton continually used an average of 739 wagons, 1,958 horses and 760 drivers.

Rivers and lakes were a vital form of transport in the war, especially as good roads were in almost as short supply as they had been in Wolfe's day, and fleets of flatboats, bateaux, sloops and other vessels were in constant use, some from Britain, many more bought, hired or seized locally.

'Officer', by Gainsborough. A flank company officer of the 4th Foot, c. 1770, is shown in campaign dress in this painting, now in the National Gallery of Victoria. Grenadier and light infantry officers wore bearskins and caps or helmets respectively, but the normal cocked hat seems to have been worn extensively, presumably to save the more expensive special headgear from hard wear in the field. The uniform has dark blue facings, a silver epaulette, silver buttons, a silver gorget, and a silver swordbelt plate engraved with a crown and 'IVth'. Note that the lapels are partly buttoned across.

The organization, 3,000 miles from home, needed for such enterprises was so vast that the wonder is that the system worked as well as it did. There was so much incompetence in the administration of the army at home that honest, efficient men have often despaired, yet even a good administrative machine would have been hard put to it to organize the conquest of the Americans in a country of such vast distances, and where so little food could be obtained – usually by fair money – from the land. The redcoats often starved and sometimes froze in their ragged uniforms. Washington's valiant men at Valley Forge may have been the champions in the misery stakes, but there were plenty of British challengers.

Starvation could sometimes be warded off by plunder. Yet the record of British troops, especially when compared with continental armies of the day, was good in America, as every reputable American has always agreed. This was partly due to the attitude of the British commanders. Howe, Burgoyne and others demanded high standards of conduct, which naturally could not always be maintained – Tory 'cowboys' sold stolen livestock to Burgoyne's army. But because Briton was fighting Briton it was regarded as vital that thieves, rapists and marauders should be discouraged. Private Thomas MacMahan of the 43rd got 1,000 lashes for receiving stolen goods in Boston in 1776 and his wife got 100 lashes and three months in prison; and two privates of the 59th were hanged for robbing a store.

There was no stopping crime, of course, especially with so many criminals in the ranks. The German mercenaries naturally had no great interest in the sensibilities of the local population and, though not the monsters of legend, were notorious for their plundering in New York and on Long Island and around Trenton. Howe simply could not stop this, nor could he control some of his newly arrived and more bloodthirsty officers. The Hessians had a reputation as butchers of surrendered troops in 1776, but they were sometimes put up to it by the British. One officer wrote: 'We took care to tell the Hessians that the Rebels had resolved to give no quarters to them in particular, which made them fight desperately and put all to death that fell into their hands. You know all strategems are lawful in war, especially against such vile enemies to their King and country.' After such a brutal sentiment, it may seem optimistic to claim that the American Revolution was a 'Gentlemen's War', yet except where it was a civil war between Patriots and Loyalists in remoter areas, that is exactly what it often was. Occasionally, in the heat of battle or the moment of surrender, revenge and misunderstanding might provoke a near atrocity; but this was a war where Colonel Simcoe, the brilliant British commander of the Loyalist Queen's Rangers, could send a

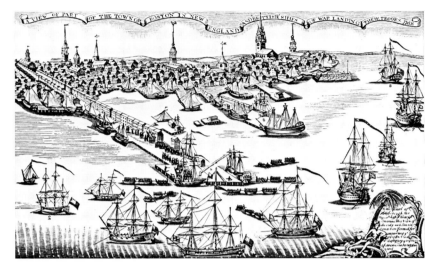

An engraving by Paul Revere showing the landing of British troops at Boston, 1768. (Michael D. Robson)

CHARLES TOWN

BOSTON

An engraving of 1790 showing the attack on Bunker Hill (Breed's Hill) by British infantry, supported by fire from warships; Charles Town is bombarded and ablaze. (Michael D. Robson)

message to an enemy sentry telling him that he would be shot if he did not retire, and shout to an American officer: 'You are a brave fellow, but you must go away.' Americans can cite the tough tactics of Banastre Tarleton in the South, but by the standards of warfare in that or any age, the American Revolution was mainly unbarbaric.

The frontier saw raids by Tories and Indians out of Niagara, but this was the civil war situation referred to above. It was also good tactics, for Butler's Rangers and Joseph Brant's Iroquois by devastating the Mohawk Valley reduced Washington's army to a state of near-starvation. Both sides tried to use Indians, but few sided with the land-hungry Colonists. As allies they varied in usefulness and quality, but they would have said the same about the British as allies. Their use inflamed public opinion in America and in Britain, but they could never have remained neutral. The fabulous, well-educated Joseph Brant, a Mohawk who knew Boswell, George III and the Prince of Wales, was their finest leader. He was

Sir John Caldwell in Indian costume, c. 1780. This officer, who served at Detroit with the 8th (King's) Regiment of Foot, acquired this magnificent example of Ojibway chief's dress when he spent some time among the Indians, organizing them for raids on the Americans and leading them in action. Dyed ostrich and peacock plumes (trade items) crown his turbaned head, and silver brooches and 'tinkling cones' decorate head and shoulders. The pipe-tomahawk and short sword were both popular trade items, and the shirt clearly came from the same source. Breech-cloth and leggings are red, the latter with a light blue tape, and the blanket is red and blue. He wears four silver gorgets, and silver ear and nose ornaments; in his hand is a belt of wampum. (Courtesy, City of Liverpool Museums)

continually with the seventy or so Loyalist regiments. Being Britons and ordinary humans, they had mixed views on their allies. Some soldiers who detested scalping – encouraged by whites as evidence 'of death – were quite prepared to view or administer 1,500 lashes. Each to his own atrocity: the slow burning at the stake, the flogging to death. . . .

Even discounting Rebel propaganda, there were plenty of instances of rape, for which redcoats could be court-martialled. The Hessians were less subject to military punishment for the crime.

The most famous quotation on the subject was penned by Lord Francis Rawdon. It defies comment except to note that for once the redcoats were being properly fed: 'The fair nymphs of this isle [Staten Island] are in wonderful tribulation, as the fresh meat our men have got here has made them riotous as satyrs. A girl cannot step into the bushes to pluck a rose without running the most imminent risk of being ravished, and they are so little accustomed to these vigorous methods they don't bear them with the proper resignation, and of consequence we have the most entertaining court-martials every day.'

Women followed the flag in disputed numbers. Howe allowed six to every company in 1776 and 1777, while Burgoyne had three per company for his expedition. He always denied that there were 2,000 women on that campaign. Like Howe, he had a mistress to console him (and, according to the wife of the Hessian commander, Baroness von Riedesel, in her marvellous account of the ill-fated march which ended at Saratoga, he had the bottle as well towards the end). But few eighteenth-century commanders were more loved by their men than 'Gentleman Johnny', not least, perhaps, because he was no great flogger and was known to mention common soldiers in dispatches.

Women, whether wives or 'wives', acted as laundrymaids and sometimes as nurses on campaign. They and their children were fed from the public stores, and clothed as well. There was at least one near mutiny at Cork when a ship without women did not set out because the redcoats aboard threatened to desert unless the matter was put right.

Sadly little is known of the ordinary women who went to America. Ironically, the best-known

reviled thanks to Rebel propaganda and natural enmity, but had nothing to reproach himself with at the end of the war except a terrible November day when he and Walter Butler lost control of their Indian followers at Cherry Valley. As for the alleged massacre of Wyoming, it was a straight victory by Walter's father, John Butler, with no women or children killed. Brant, execrated for his part in it, was not even present!

Redcoats often fought alongside Indians and

woman of the Revolution on the British side was the unfortunate Jane McCrae, famous because she was murdered by some of Burgoyne's Indians, who neither knew nor cared that she was a Loyalist, due to marry a Loyalist officer. Her cruel death was turned to maximum advantage by the Americans, with justification; yet the worst incident of the entire Revolutionary period was committed by American frontier militia who, systematically and in cold blood, butchered some 100 Christian Delawares, men, women and children.

A worse fate than being butchered awaited many prisoners on both sides. Just as in the Civil War one is confronted by the nobility of Robert E. Lee and the horror of Andersonville prison camp, so in the Revolution the decency of many British leaders is in striking contrast to the terrible prison hulks off New York, where perhaps 7,000 Americans perished in utter squalor and misery. And the redcoats (and especially the Loyalists) suffered almost as badly. The Americans imprisoned some of the latter in the nightmarish Simsbury copper mines. Fortunately, the redcoats suffered less because the Americans had fewer prison facilities.

Not that that can excuse the shameful treatment accorded to Burgoyne's surrendered army. His victor's very generous terms were quashed by Congress, but it has since come to light that Howe was eager to use the men again rather than, as the treaty specified, have them sent back to Britain, which puts both sides in the wrong. But Congress did not know of Howe's secret letter to Burgoyne, whose men first endured harsh treatment in New England, then were marched south,

The 'Massacre of Wyoming', Pennsylvania, in 1778, was actually a victory for Colonel John Butler and his Rangers and Indians; it was built up by propaganda and rumour into 'the surpassing horror of the Revolution'. Joseph Brant shared the blame for it, although he was not even present at the battle. Nevertheless, Alonzo Chappel's painting gives a vivid enough picture of frontier warfare. (Courtesy, Chicago Historical Society)

partly to make the men desert – which many Hessians did – and were finally quartered in Virginia. Many, like Sergeant Lamb, escaped, a few redcoats deserted, and the rest remained loyal until, in 1781, they were separated from their officers and vanished from history. How many of the original 3,000 redcoats disappeared is uncertain.

Many of the Hessians and some of the redcoats who did desert no doubt settled down to a new life in America. The war saw hundreds of deserters, only a small percentage of them redcoats, but not so many traitors in the conventional sense. Naturally, the Loyalists regarded all Rebels as traitors, and vice versa, and it could be argued that many of the Opposition in London were traitors! But in the full sense of the word, of men who betrayed their side as opposed to changing sides in the manner inevitable in a civil war, there were few, the most notable being the Rebels' best general, Benedict Arnold.

Hospitals on the American side were much worse than British ones. Not all can have been as bad as Ticonderoga's in 1776, which 'beggars description and shocks humanity', as Anthony Wayne wrote. But the general standard must have been in stark contrast to the British ones. Dr Rush, a signatory of the Declaration of Independence, paid a fulsome tribute in a letter to John Adams about Howe's hospitals and his doctors, even stressing that wounded American prisoners were much better looked after by the British (before going to the hulks?) than the wounded in American hospitals. The British 'pay a supreme regard to the cleanliness and health of their men', wrote the doctor after his inspection, and contrasted American hospitals most unfavourably.

Of course, temporary hospitals on campaign must have been akin to butchers' shops, and it must not be supposed that the chances of recovery from serious wounds could ever be high in the 1770s and 1780s; but this tribute is significant, not least because it shows Howe's concern for his men, which made him such a popular commander. Rush even paid a tribute to the British for filling their men with vegetables. Regimental doctors many of whom were most dedicated, were paid so badly that some bought an extra commission and fought as well as healed.

Disease was a greater killer in the war than battle, though, strangely, British casualties are not known. The American figures are mere guesswork, perhaps 12,000 killed, which may be not so different to the number of British deaths in action. It was not a very sanguine war.

When the war finally ended the redcoats had the rare and unpleasant experience of sailing away defeated despite many victories, in contrast to the more usual British technique of ultimate victories after disastrous early campaigns. Their record was good, for honours could have included Long Island, White Plains, Fort Washington, Brandywine, Germantown, Savannah, Charleston, Camden and Guilford. Saratoga and Yorktown, those crucial defeats, were lost because strategy, communications and liaison were at fault. Though the war was frequently fought on the European pattern, rigid formations often gave way to looser, more open tactics.

The very finest units were both Loyalist formations, led by British Regulars, Simcoe's Queen's Rangers and Tarleton's British Legion, as dashing mounted troops as have ever served the crown. The infantry fought in two ranks, in open order. In the pitched battles of Brandywine, Camden and Guilford, the redcoats, infantry and gunners excelled themselves, while all the four leading British commanders, Howe, Burgoyne, Clinton and Cornwallis, were usually (after Bunker Hill) able, if not inspired.

As for the redcoat, 200 years on, and despite Sir John Fortescue's *History of the British Army*, and the writings of friendly Americans and understanding native historians, his achievement, courage and famous discipline in adversity in the Revolution will probably never get its due. It was not he who lost George III his American Colonies. Memorials to him are few, but there is one near the spot where the war began, which commemorates those who fell at Concord Bridge. It is quaint, perhaps, but none the worse for that – and it was written in sincerity and by the enemy:

> They came three thousand miles and died,
> To keep the past upon the throne;
> Unheard, beyond the ocean tide,
> Their English mother made her moan.

A Diary of the American Revolution

1775

19 Apr.   Battle of Lexington and Concord, ending in fighting retreat by the British to Boston.

17 June   Battle of Breed's Hill/Bunker Hill. 'A dear bought victory,' wrote Clinton, 'another such would have ruined us.'

3 July   Washington takes command of American Army.

4 Sept.– Siege and loss of St John's.
3 Nov.

10 Oct.   Sir William Howe succeeds Gage as C.-in-C. in America. Carleton given command in Canada.

17 Oct.   Fall of Chambly after a short siege.

13 Nov.   Americans under Montgomery occupy Montreal.

4 Dec.   Americans besiege Quebec.

9 Dec.   Great Bridge, Virginia. British troops defeated.

1776

27 Feb.   Moore's Creek Bridge, North Carolina. Severe Loyalist defeat.

17 Mar.   British evacuate Boston.

5 May   Relief of Quebec, Carleton and his men having saved Canada.

16 May   Battle of the Cedars. Americans defeated by Indians, plus some Canadians and redcoats.

June–   Carleton frees northern New York, but
Oct.   does not risk attacking Ticonderoga and retires to St John's for the winter.

4 June–   British campaign in South Carolina.
21 July   Failure of attack on Charleston.

4 July   Declaration of Independence.

Aug.–   British campaign in New York and New
Dec.   Jersey.

27 Aug.   British victory on Long Island.

15 Sept. Battle of Harlem Heights. British victory but heavy casualties. Howe occupies New York.

11 Oct.   Battle on Lake Champlain. Brave fight by Benedict Arnold and a scratch fleet ends in British victory.

18 Oct.   Sharp delaying action by Americans at Pell's Point, New York.

28 Oct.   Battle of White Plains, New York. Indecisive victory.

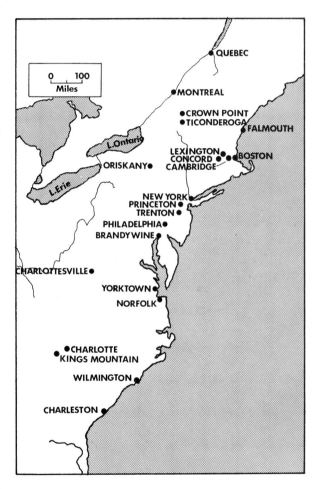

16 Nov.   Fort Washington, New York, falls to British.

25–26   Washington crosses the Delaware and
Dec.   defeats Hessians at Trenton, one of the Revolution's turning-points, because it impresses Europeans, besides raising his own men's morale.

21

Eighteenth-century view of American troops: 'a rifleman' and 'a general'. (Michael D. Robson)

22 Oct.	British fail to capture Fort Mercer.
15 Nov.	Fort Mifflin taken by British.
18 Dec.	Washington in winter quarters at Valley Forge.

1778

6 Feb.	Franco-American alliance signed.
24 May	Clinton takes over from Howe as C.-in-C.
28 June	Battle of Monmouth. Indecisive. Last major engagement in the North.
4 July	Butler's Rangers and Indians victory at Wyoming, Pennsylvania, wrongly claimed by Americans to be an atrocity.
29 Aug.	Failure of French and Americans to take Rhode Island.
11 Nov.	Cherry Valley Massacre. Walter Butler and Brant fail to control their Indians.
29 Dec.	British take Savannah.

1777

3 Jan.	Americans take Princeton, New Jersey.
1 Feb.–9 May	Minor campaigning in New Jersey.
1 July	Beginning of Burgoyne's campaign.
5 July	Rebels evacuate Ticonderoga.
6 Aug.	Ferocious battle at Oriskany between British, Loyalists and Indians versus Rebels. A bloody victory. Indians under Joseph Brant.
22 Aug.	Siege of Fort Stanwix (Schuyler) ends in failure, thus finishing St Leger's sweep from the West along the Mohawk to assist Burgoyne.
16 Aug.	Germans defeated at Bennington.
11 Sept.	Howe defeats Washington at Brandywine Creek.
19 Sept.	Battle of Freeman's Farm. British win costly fight.
20 Sept.	Americans attacked at Paoli.
26 Sept.	Howe takes Philadelphia.
7 Oct.	Battle of Bemis Heights (or second battle of Freeman's Farm). Another near-disastrous British action. Arnold distinguishes himself.
17 Oct.	Burgoyne surrenders at Saratoga. The turning-point of the Revolution.

1779

Jan.	Capture of Sunbury and Augusta by British.
23 Feb.	Culmination of brilliant campaign in the West by George Rogers Clark when Vincennes falls.
Mar.–June	Bitter civil war in the South.
8 May	Spain declares war on Britain.
15 July	Wayne captures Stony Point from British.
13 Aug.	Disastrous Massachusetts attack on Penobscot Bay.
29 Aug.	Sullivan's expedition, sent to destroy the towns of the Six Nations (Iroquois), defeats them at Newtown, New York, and burns their crops and homes.
9 Oct.	French and Americans fail to take Savannah.
26 Dec.	British fleet sails to attack Charleston.

1780

14 Mar.	Fall of Mobile to Spaniards.
12 May	British capture Charleston.
11 July	French troops arrive at Newport, Rhode Island.

Major John André of the 54th Foot, *c.* 1779 – the year before he was hanged as a spy by the Americans after conducting secret negotiations with their treacherous general, Benedict Arnold. André died with magnificent courage in front of a crowd of admiring and grieving enemies. Born in Switzerland in 1751, he joined the army in 1771 and rose to be Clinton's adjutant-general. (Courtesy the Curator, Dorset Military Museum)

1782

23 Feb.	Carleton becomes C.-in-C., replacing Clinton.
Mar.–Aug.	Bitter frontier warfare continues.
12 Apr.	Rodney defeats French fleet in West Indies.
11 July	Savannah abandoned by British.
30 Nov.	First peace treaty signed in Paris.
14 Dec.	British evacuate Charleston.

1783

19 Apr.	End of hostilities proclaimed by Congress.
3 Sept.	Final peace treaty signed.
25 Nov.	Main British evacuation of New York.
23 Dec.	George Washington stands down.

16 Aug.	Battle of Camden. Total defeat of Americans under Gates.
25 Sept.	Treason of Benedict Arnold.
2 Oct.	Hanging of Major André.
7 Oct.	British and Loyalists under Ferguson defeated at King's Mountain.

1781

17 Jan.	Morgan defeats British under Tarleton at the Cowpens.
15 Mar.	Greene and Cornwallis fight indecisive battle at Guilford Court House. Heavy casualties.
25 Apr.	Hobkirk's Hill. Rawdon wins another expensive victory.
June	By the end of June, British power in the Carolinas broken.
8 Sept.	Battle of Eutaw Springs. Greene defeats British, who retreat to Charleston.
28 Sept.	Washington and Rochambeau march from Williamsburg towards Yorktown.
6 Oct.	British besieged.
19 Oct.	Cornwallis surrenders at Yorktown.

Contemporary view of the surrender of Lord Cornwallis to American and French forces at Yorktown, 1781. (Michael D. Robson)

The Regiments Which Served

(with modern designations before the amalgamations of the 1960s)

No.	Name	Modern Name	Arrival	Departure	Facings
3rd	Buffs	The Buffs (Royal East Kent Regiment)	June 1781 Charleston	1782 West Indies	Buff
4th	King's Own	King's Own Royal Regiment (Lancaster)	June 1774 Boston	1778 West Indies	Blue
5th		Royal Northumberland Fusiliers	July 1774 Boston	1778 West Indies	Green
6th		Royal Warwickshire Regiment	October 1776 New York	1776 Drafted	Yellow
7th	Royal Fusiliers	Royal Fusiliers (City of London Regiment)	July 1773 Canada	1783 British Isles	Blue
8th	King's	King's (Liverpool) Regiment	1768 Canada	1785 British Isles	Blue
9th		Royal Norfolk Regiment	May 1776 Quebec	1777 Interned	Yellow
10th		Royal Lincolnshire Regiment	1767 Canada	1778 Drafted	Yellow
14th		West Yorkshire Regiment (Prince of Wales's Own)	1766 Halifax	1777 Drafted	Buff
15th		East Yorkshire Regiment (Duke of York's Own)	May 1776 Cape Fear	1778 West Indies	Yellow
16th		Bedfordshire and Hertfordshire Regiment	1767 New York	1782 Drafted	Yellow
17th		Royal Leicestershire Regiment	December 1775 Boston	1781 Interned	White
18th	Royal Irish	Royal Irish Regiment (disbanded 1922)	1767 Philadelphia	1775 Drafted	Blue
19th		Green Howards (Alexandra Princess of Wales's Own Yorkshire Regiment)	June 1781 Charleston	1782 West Indies	Green
20th		Lancashire Fusiliers	May 1776 Quebec	1777 Interned	Yellow
21st	Royal North British Fusiliers	Royal Scots Fusiliers	May 1776 Quebec	1777 Interned	Blue
22nd		Cheshire Regiment	July 1775 Boston	1783 British Isles	Buff
23rd	Royal Welsh Fusiliers	Royal Welch Fusiliers	1773 New York	1781 Interned	Blue
24th		South Wales Borderers	May 1776 Quebec	1777 Interned	Green
26th	Cameronians	Cameronians (Scottish Rifles)	1767 New Jersey	1779 Drafted	Yellow

1 **Private, Light Company, 38th Foot**
2 **Corporal, Grenadier Company, 47th Foot**
3 **Private, Battalion Company, 64th Foot**

G. A. EMBLETON

A

1 Private, Battalion Company, 49th Foot, marching order
2 Drummer, 31st Foot, marching order
3 Ensign, 55th Foot, with Regimental colour

B

G. A. EMBLETON

1 Major-General in frock coat
2 Gunner, Hesse-Cassel Field
  Artillery, 1776–82
3 Officer, Royal Artillery

G. A. EMBLETON

C

1 Ensign with Regimental standard, Brunswick Infantry Regiment, von Rhetz, 1776–7
2 Grenadier, Hesse-Hanau Infantry Regiment, Erbprinz, 1776
3 Musketeer, Anhalt-Zerbst Infantry Regiment, 1781

1

2

3

D

G. A. EMBLETON

1 Corporal Foot Jägers, Hesse-Cassel
  Field Jäger Corps
2 Officer, Grenadier Company, 10th
  Foot
3 Sergeant, Battalion Company,
  29th Foot

1 **Private, 17th Light Dragoons, on service with Tarleton's British Legion**

2 **Officer, 16th (Queen's) Light Dragoons, 1776–8**

3 **Private, Brunswick Dragoon Regiment Prinz Ludwig Ernst, 1776–7**

F

G. A. EMBLETON

1 **Light Infantryman, Battle of Germantown,** 1777
2 **Private, 62nd Foot,** 1777
3 **Officer, 5th Foot,** 1777

1

2

3

G. A. EMBLETON

G

1 Officer, 42nd Royal Highland
  Regiment, 1776
2 Private, 42nd Royal Highland
  Regiment, 1783
3 Officer, Flank Company, 42nd
  Royal Highland Regiment, 1783

H

No.	Name	Modern Name	Arrival	Departure	Facings
27th	Enniskillens	Royal Inniskilling Fusiliers	October 1775 Boston	1778 West Indies	Buff
28th		Gloucestershire Regiment	May 1776 Cape Fear	1778 West Indies	Yellow
29th		Worcestershire Regiment	May 1776 Quebec	1787 British Isles	Yellow
30th		East Lancashire Regiment	June 1781 Charleston	1782 West Indies	Yellow
31st		East Surrey Regiment	May 1776 Quebec	1787 British Isles	Buff
33rd		Duke of Wellington's Regiment (West Riding)	May 1776 Cape Fear	1781 Interned	Red
34th		The Border Regiment	May 1776 Cape Fear	1786 British Isles	Yellow
35th		Royal Sussex Regiment	June 1775 Boston	1778 West Indies	Orange
37th		Royal Hampshire Regiment	May 1776 Cape Fear	1783 Left New York	Yellow
38th		South Staffordshire Regiment	July 1774 Boston	1783 Left New York	Yellow
40th		South Lancashire Regiment (Prince of Wales's Volunteers)	June 1775 Boston	1778 West Indies	Buff
42nd	Royal Highland Regiment	Black Watch (Royal Highland Regiment)	July 1776 New York	1783 Left New York	Blue
43rd		Oxford and Bucks Light Infantry	June 1774 Boston	1781 Interned	White
44th		Essex Regiment	June 1775 Boston	1780 Canada	Yellow
45th		Sherwood Foresters (Notts and Derbyshire Regiment)	July 1775 Boston	1778 Drafted	Green
46th		Duke of Cornwall's Light Infantry (2nd Battalion)	May 1776 Cape Fear	1778 West Indies	Yellow
47th		The Loyal Regiment (North Lancashire)	1773 New Jersey	1777 Interned	White
49th		Royal Berkshire Regiment (Princess Charlotte of Wales's)	June 1775 Boston	1778 West Indies	Green
52nd		Oxfordshire and Bucks Light Infantry (2nd Battalion)	October 1774 Boston	1778 Drafted	Buff
53rd		King's Shropshire Light Infantry	May 1776 Quebec	1777 Interned	Red
54th		Dorset Regiment (2nd Battalion)	May 1776 Cape Fear	1783 Left New York	Green
55th		The Border Regiment (2nd Battalion)	December 1775 Boston	1778 West Indies	Green
57th		Middlesex Regiment (Duke of Cambridge's Own)	May 1776 Cape Fear	1783 Left New York	Yellow

No.	Name	Modern Name	Arrival	Departure	Facings
59th		East Lancashire Regiment (2nd Battalion)	1765 Halifax	1775 Drafted	Red
60th	Royal American Regiment	King's Royal Rifle Corps	Many locations		Blue
62nd		Wiltshire Regiment (Duke of Edinburgh's)	May 1776 Quebec	1777 Interned	Buff
63rd		Manchester Regiment	June 1775 Boston	1782 West Indies	Green
64th		North Staffordshire Regiment (Prince of Wales's)	1768 Boston	1782 West Indies	Black
65th		York and Lancaster Regiment	1768 Boston	1776 Drafted	White
69th		Welch Regiment (2nd Battalion)	September 1781 New York	1781 West Indies	Green
70th		East Surrey Regiment (2nd Battalion)	August 1778 Halifax	1783 Canada	Black
71st	Fraser's Highlanders	Disbanded 1783	July 1776 New York	1782 Charleston	White
74th	Argyll Highlanders	Disbanded 1784	August 1778 Halifax	Canada	Yellow
76th	MacDonald's Highlanders	Disbanded 1784	1779 New York	1781 Interned	Green
80th	Royal Edinburgh Volunteers	Disbanded 1784	1779 New York	1781 Interned	Yellow
82nd	Duke of Hamilton's Regiment	Disbanded 1784	August 1778 Halifax	1782 Charleston	Black
84th	Royal Highland Emigrants	Disbanded 1784	1775 Raised in Canada as Royal Highland Emigrants. 1st Battalion stayed in Canada	1782 Charleston (2nd Battalion)	Blue
105th	King's Irish Regiment	Disbanded 1783	1778 Raised in America as Volunteers of Ireland	1782 Left Charleston	
1st	Food Guards	Grenadier Guards	July 1776 New York	1781 Interned	Blue
2nd	Coldstream Regiment of Foot Guards	Coldstream Guards	July 1776 New York	1781 Interned	Blue
3rd	Foot Guards	Scots Guards	July 1776 New York	1781 Interned	Blue
16th	Queen's Light Dragoons	16/5th Queen's Royal Lancers	July 1776 New York	1778 Drafted	Blue
17th	Light Dragoons	17/21st Lancers	June 1775 Boston	1783 British Isles	White

SOME FOOD FACTS

As described earlier, most of the food eaten by the redcoats in America had to be shipped across the Atlantic: 2,032,538 lb. of bread were received by Daniel Chamier, Commissary-General in North America between 6 February 1775 and 9 January 1778 – and 10,739 gallons of vinegar, etc. Here is one account in full:

ACCOUNT OF PROVISIONS RECEIVED BY COMMISSARY-GENERAL DANIEL WEIR AT NEW YORK BETWEEN 7 OCT. 1774 AND 5 SEPT. 1781.

Kind of Provision	Amount	Value		
		£	s.	d.
Bread	512,182 lb.	4,020	9	6
Spirits	42,655 gals.	5,687	7	0
Beef	42,832 lb.	2,699	6	2
Pork	83,269 lb.	3,469	11	1¾
Flour	164,884 lb.	1,099	10	8
Raisins	2,574 lb.	45	19	3
Pease	1,148 bush.	242	9	2
Oatmeal	12,007 gals.	422	14	1
Rice	91,557 lb.	897	5	1½
Oil	2,385 gals.	531	15	4¼
Butter	14,516 lb.	463	14	6½
Cheese	251 lb.	3	10	7½
Vinegar	4,618 gals.	125	0	2
Casks	1,052 tuns	1,778	2	1
Hoops	12,233			
Bags	3,994	216	6	10
Jars	84	42	0	0
Candles	120 doz.	40	5	0
Sauerkraut	123 barr.	215	5	9
		£22,000	12	5½

Quoting a soldier's daily ration is more hazardous than a provisions' list like the one above, for the obvious reason that the delivery of provisions to armies or regiments or detachments was bound to be erratic. Nathaniel Day, Commissary-General in Canada, wrote to Burgoyne on 31 May 1777 that the Treasury Board had ordered one man's rations per day to be as follows:

1 lb. Bread or Flour
1 lb. Beef or 9 and one-seventh oz. pork
Three-sevenths pints pease
Six-sevenths oz. Butter or in lieu 1 one-seventh oz.
    Cheese 2 two-sevenths oz. flour or in lieu 1
    one-seventh oz. Rice or 1 one-seventh oz.
    Oatmeal.

Like the Royal Navy, the redcoats enjoyed a rum ration, usually diluted. It was up to commanding generals what other drinks were issued. These included claret, porter and spruce beer, the latter being most popular as it did not entail pay stoppages. As for patients in hospitals, here is an official menu for 1778–81:

Full Diet
Breakfast
Rice gruel, or Water Gruel, with Sugar or Butter
Dinner
One Pound of Fresh Meat: Viz: Beef, Mutton, or Veal, with Greens
Supper
Two ounces of Butter, or Cheese
Half Diet
Dinner
Rice, and Pudding, and half a Pound of Fresh Meat; four times a week
Breakfast & Supper, as Full Diet
Low Diet
Breakfast, and Supper, Rice or Water Gruel; Milk; Porridge, Sago or Salop
Dinner
Broth & Pudding

One Pound of Bread; each Man per Diem, with three pints of Spruce Beer in Summer and a Quart in Winter.
Rice Water: for common drink in Fluxes; and Barley in Fevers . . .

A typical example of the rather splendid Light Dragoon helmet of the day. (National Army Museum)

Lieutenant Thomas Aubrey of the 4th Foot, *c.* 1771; a portrait by Nathaniel Hone. Again, the scarlet coat faced dark blue is trimmed with silver 'metal'. Note the construction of the unstiffened epaulette – a flat knot of silver lace braid. (**By permission of the National Museum of Wales**)

It cannot be stressed too strongly once again that for all the talk of rations per man there was a constant shortage of food and that much of it was rotten – uneatable even in those tough times and unthinkable to us today. Surveyors checked the food when it left Cork and when it reached America and kept finding such items as 'very old Bread, Weavile Eaten, full of Maggots, mouldy, musty and rotten and entirely unfit for men to eat'. To end with, here is a classic quotation of life aboard a transport. All honour to redcoats, Hessians and Loyalists who fought like lions even on empty bellies, and to those who sailed to America under conditions like these:

'Pork and pease were the chief of their diet. The pork seemed to be four or five years old. It was streaked with black towards the outside and was yellow farther in, with a little white in the middle. The salt beef was in much the same condition. The ship biscuit was so hard that they sometimes broke it up with a canonball, and the story ran that it had been taken from the French in the Seven Years War and lain in Portsmouth ever since . . . Sometimes they had groats and barley, or, by way of a treat a pudding made of flour mixed half with salt water and half with fresh water, and with old mutton fat.'

ARMY ADMINISTRATION

During the American Revolution the army was still legalized annually by a Mutiny Act passed by Parliament. The following is a brief breakdown of the English establishment.

Captain-General – The King
Commander-in-Chief – Vacant 1772–78
Sir Jeffrey Amherst 1778–82
Secretary at War – Viscount Barrington

Lord Barrington's was the key post, especially, of course, before Amherst was appointed. An able man, his duties were manifold. It is interesting that, like so many others, he sympathized with the Americans.

THE WAR OFFICE

Secretary at War – Viscount Barrington
Deputy Secretary and First Clerk – Matthew Lewis
(who had ten or so clerks)
Paymaster of Widows' Pensions – Hon. Henry Fox
Deputy – John Powell
Examiner of Army Accounts – William Smith
Assistant – Z. R. Taylor

THE PAYMASTER-GENERAL'S OFFICE, 1775

Paymaster-General – Rt. Hon. Richard Rigby, M.P.
Deputy Paymaster-General – Anthony Sawyer
Accountant – John Powell
Computer of Off-reckonings – Charles Bembridge
Cashier of Half Pay – Robert Randall
Keeper of the Stores – P. Burrell

Also eight clerks. There were eight subordinate paymasters abroad. The office of paymaster-general was the equivalent of being given a licence to print money.

CIVIL BRANCH OF THE OFFICE OF ORDNANCE

Master-General – Rt. Hon. Geo. Viscount Townshend
Lieutenant-General – Sir Jeffrey Amherst, K.B.
Surveyor-General – Sir C. Frederick, K.B., F.R.S.
Clerk of the Ordnance – Sir Chas. Cocks, Bart.
Storekeeper – Andrew Wilkinson

Clerk of the Deliveries – Benjamin Langlois, Esq.
Treasurer and Paymaster – John Ross Mackye, Esq.
Secretary to the Master-General – John Courtney, Esq.
Under-secretary to the Master-General – T. Masterson, Esq.
Minuting Clerk – H. Simmonds
There were also eight clerks.

MILITARY BRANCH OF THE OFFICE OF ORDNANCE

Chief Engineer and Colonel – Lieutenant-General W. Skinner
Directors and Lieutenant-Colonels – Colonel James Montréssor, Lieutenant-Colonel Arch. Patoun
Sub. Directors and Majors – Four in number
Engineers in Ord. and Captains – Twelve in number.
Engineers Extra. and Captains and Lieutenants – Twelve in number
Practitioner Engineers and Designs – Sixteen in number

The Ordnance Department was in charge of everything from arms and ammunition to prisons and maps and controlled the gunners, sappers and Woolwich Military Academy. Both the army and navy depended on its efficiency and rules. Townshend was the thorn in Wolfe's flesh at Quebec and Amherst the final conqueror of Canada.

Among other functionaries were the Judge Advocate-General, the Apothecary-General and the Comptroller of Army Accounts, and there were various other boards, notably the Treasury which fed and equipped the army, and the Admiralty Board. There was also a board of officers to advise the King and the Secretary at War, thirty strong. It sat when required and discussed commissions, abuses, pay, courts martial and many other matters. And the clothing board had, as its name suggests, to decide on uniform patterns and inspect them. Though the general officers did not make contracts – this was left to colonels and regimental agents – they approved them. There was also a board which ran Chelsea Hospital. Troops were affected by the Navy Board and victualling boards when they sailed on transports.

At first glance, these lists may seem impressive, but there was far too much overlapping and not enough central authority. The result was often a shambles, and this affected the outcome of the war.

The Royal Warrant of 1768 for Infantry Clothing, Colours &c.

(*not including the devices and badges of the Royal Regiments, and of the six Old Corps*)

GEORGE R.

Our will and pleasure is, that the following regulations for the colours, clothing, &c. of Our marching regiments of foot, be duly observed and put in execution, at such times as the particulars are or shall be furnished.

No Colonel is to put his arms, crest, device, or livery, on any part of the appointments of the regiment under his command.

Colours

The King's, or first colour of every regiment, is to be the Great Union throughout.

The second Colour to be the colour of the facing of the regiment, with the Union in the upper canton; except those regiments which are faced with red, white, or black. The second colour of those regiments which are faced with red or white, is to be the red cross of St. George in a white field, and the Union in the upper canton. The second colour of those which are faced with black, is to be St. George's cross throughout; Union in the upper canton; the three other cantons, black.

In the centre of each colour is to be painted, or embroidered, in gold Roman characters, the number of the rank of the regiment, within the wreath of roses and thistles on the same stalk; except those regiments which are allowed to wear any royal devices, or ancient badges; on whose colours the rank of the regiment is to be painted, or embroidered, towards the upper corner. The size of the colours to be six feet six inches flying, and six feet deep on the pike. The length of the pike (spear and ferril included) to be nine feet ten inches. The cords and tassels of the whole to be crimson and gold mixed.

Drums

The drums to be wood.

The front to be painted with the colour of the

facing of the regiment, with the King's cypher and crown, and the number of the regiment under it.

Bells of Arms
The bells of arms to be painted in the same manner.

Camp Colours
The camp colours to be eighteen inches square, and of the colour of the facing of the regiment, with the number of the regiment upon them. The poles to be seven feet six inches long, except those of the Quarter and rear guards, which are to be nine feet.

Uniform of Officers
The number of each regiment to be on the buttons of the uniforms of the Officers and men. The coats to be lappelled to the waist with the colour of the regiment, and the colour not to be varied from what is particularly specified hereafter. They may be without embroidery or lace; but, if the Colonel thinks proper, either gold or silver embroidered or laced button-holes are permitted. To have cross pockets, and sleeves with round cuffs, and no slits. The lappels and cuffs to be of the same breadth as is ordered for the men.

Epaulettes
The Officers of grenadiers to wear an epaulette on each shoulder. Those of the battalion to wear one on the right shoulder. They are to be either of embroidery or lace, with gold or silver fringe.

Waistcoats
The waistcoats to be plain, without either embroidery or lace.

Swords and Sword-Knots
The swords of each regiment to be uniform, and the sword-knots of the whole to be crimson and gold in stripes. The hilts of the swords to be either gilt or silver, according to the colour of the buttons on the uniforms.

Hats
The hats to be laced either with gold or silver, as hereafter specified, and to be cocked uniformly.

Sashes and Gorgets
The sashes to be of crimson silk, and worn round the waist. The King's arms to be engraved on the gorgets; also the number of the regiment. They are to be either gilt or silver, according to the colour of the buttons on the uniforms. The badges of those regiments which are entitled to any, are also to be engraved.

Caps, Fuzils, and Pouches, for Grenadier Officers
The Officers of the grenadiers to wear black bearskin caps; and to have fuzils, shoulder-belts, and pouches. The shoulder-belts to be white or buff, according to the colour of their waistcoats.

Espontoons
The battalion officers to have espontoons.

Gaiters
The whole to have black linen gaiters, with black buttons, and small stiff tops, black garters, and uniform buckles.

Serjeants' Coats
The coats of the Serjeants to be lappelled to the waist, with the colour of the facing of the regiment. The button-holes of the coat to be of white braid. Those on the waistcoats to be plain. The Serjeants of grenadiers to have fuzils, pouches, and caps. Those of the battalion to have halberts, and no pouches.

Serjeants' Sashes
The sashes to be of crimson worsted, with a stripe of the colour of the facing of the regiment, and worn round the waist. Those of the regiments which are faced with red, to have a stripe of white.

Corporals' Coats
The coats of the Corporals to have a silk epaulette on the right shoulder.

Grenadiers' Coats
The coats of the grenadiers to have the usual round wings of red cloth on the point of the shoulder, with six loops of the same sort of lace as on the button-holes, and a border round the bottom.

Private Men's Coats
The men's coats to be looped with worsted lace, but no border. The ground of the lace to be white, with coloured stripes. To have white buttons. The breadth of the lace which is to make the loop round the button-hole, to be about half an inch. Four loops to be on the sleeves, and four on the pockets, with two on each side of the slit behind.

Lappels, Sleeves, and Pockets
The breadth of all the lappels to be three inches, to reach down to the waist, and not to be wider at top than at the bottom. The sleeves of the coats to have a small round cuff, without any slit, and to be made so that they may be unbuttoned and let down. The

whole to have cross pockets, but no flaps to those of the waistcoat. The cuffs of the sleeve which turns up, to be three inches and a half deep. The flap on the pocket of the coat to be sewed down, and the pocket to be cut in the lining of the coat.

Shoulder Belts and Waist Belts

The breadth of the shoulder-belts to be two inches and three-quarters; that of the waist-belt to be two inches; and those regiments which have buff waistcoats, are to have buff-coloured accoutrements. Those which have white waistcoats, are to have white.

Drummers' and Fifers' Coats

The coats of the drummers and fifers of all the royal regiments are to be red, faced and lappelled with blue, and laced with royal lace. The waistcoats, breeches, and lining of the coats, to be of the same colour as that which is ordered for their respective regiments. The coats of the drummers and fifers of those regiments which are faced with red, are to be white, faced, lappelled, and lined with red; red waistcoats and breeches. Those of all the other regiments are to be colour of the facing of their regiments; faced and lappelled with red. The waistcoats, breeches, and lining of those which have buff or white coats, are to be red. Those of all the others are to be of the same colour as that which is ordered for the men. To be laced in such manner as the Colonel shall think fit. The lace to be of the colour of that of the soldiers' coats. The coats to have no hanging sleeves behind.

Drummers' and Fifers' Caps

The drummers and fifers to have black bear-skin caps. On the front, the King's crest, of silver plated metal, on a black ground, with trophies of colours and drums. The number of the regiment on the back part; as also the badge, if entitled to any, as ordered for the grenadiers.

Grenadiers' Caps

The caps of the grenadiers to be of black bear-skin. On the front, the King's crest, of silver plated metal, on a black ground, with the motto, *Nec aspera terrent*. A grenade on the back part, with the number of the regiment on it. The royal regiments, and the six old corps, are to have the crest and grenade, and also the other particulars as hereafter specified. The badge of the royal regiments is to be white, and set on near the top of the back part of the cap. The height of the cap (without the bear-skin, which reaches beyond the top) to be twelve inches.

Hats of the Whole

The hats of the Serjeants to be laced with silver. Those of the Corporals and private men to have a white tape binding. The breadth of the whole to be one inch and a quarter; and no more to be on the back part of the brim, than what is necessary to sew it down. To have black cockades.

Caps for the Officers and Men of Regiments of Fuzileers

The regiments of fuzileers to have black bear-skin caps. They are to be made in the same manner as those which are ordered for the grenadiers, but not so high; and not to have the grenade on the back part.

Swords

All the Serjeants of the regiment, and the whole grenadier company, to have swords. The Corporals and private men of the battalion companies (excepting the regiment of royal highlanders) to have no swords.

All the drummers and fifers to have a short sword with a scimitar blade.

Gaiters

The Serjeants, Corporals, drummers, fifers, and private men, to have black gaiters of the same sort as is ordered for the Officers; also black garters and uniform buckles.

Pioneers

Each pioneer to have an axe, a saw, and an apron; a cap with a leather crown, and a black bear-skin front, on which is to be the King's crest in white on a red ground; also an axe and a saw. The number of the regiment to be on the back part of the cap.

A leather cap, almost certainly a light infantry type of *c.* 1775, with a small visor or peak which could be turned down to protect the eyes. (National Army Museum)

The Plates

A1 Private, Light Company, 38th Foot

The 38th, later the South Staffordshire Regiment, had yellow facings, and silver lace for officers. It served throughout the War of Independence, notably at Lexington, Breed's Hill, Long Island, Fort Lee, Chestnut Neck, Brandywine, Germantown, and Monmouth Courthouse.

Light troops had been used in America during the French and Indian War, and some regiments had 'picket' and 'Highland' companies; but in 1771 a light company was officially added to each regiment. Active and agile men were preferred, and their training laid some stress on initiative. The light companies of a number of regiments serving together were often detached into a separate light battalion; sometimes the light and grenadier companies of several regiments would be grouped in an élite formation. Light company men were to wear short jackets with shoulder-wings, red waistcoats, and short black gaiters. A black leather cap with three chains round it and a piece of plate upon the centre of the crown, like a skull-cap, was distinguished by the regimental number and the royal cipher beneath a crown on a large round peak standing straight up in front. A large variety of caps were made, or cut down from cocked hats: some had peaks in front, others at the back, some had horsehair crests, others were made of leather and brass like dragoon helmets. The men carried a small cartridge-box on a tan leather waistbelt, a powder horn and bullet pouch, and a hatchet and bayonet in a frog; sometimes the hatchet had a single case buttoning round the blade. Officers and sergeants carried fusils (light muskets) and pouches.

A2 Corporal, Grenadier Company, 47th Foot

The 47th, later the Loyal Regiment, wore white facings; two black lines were added to the design of the regimental lace of corporals and men, in mourning for General Wolfe. The regiment fought with Burgoyne's army, and was interned with the rest of that unlucky command in 1777.

The Grenadier Company, though no longer issued with actual grenades, was composed of the largest and strongest men in each battalion, and provided a shock force. It was often detached and formed into separate grenadier battalions (see above), to the disgust of many officers, who held that to draw off each battalion's best men in this way was a distortion of their proper function and weakened their parent unit unreasonably. This corporal – his rank distinguished by the knot on his right shoulder, although corporals in some regiments wore a white silk epaulette – wears a uniform conforming to the 1768 Clothing Warrant quoted in the body of the text. The distinctions peculiar to the Grenadier Company of the battalion are the fur cap, the shoulder-wings decorated with regimental lace loops, the brass match-case on the crossbelt, and the sword: this latter was only carried by grenadiers, sergeants and officers by this date. It is also possible that a tightly coiled and pipe-clayed match was fixed to the crossbelt behind the shoulder, as another reminder of the original function. The expensive fur cap was covered on the march with a painted canvas cover; when not in use these could be rolled up and suspended by a small loop from the right hip coat button, concealed within the tuck of the skirts. In peacetime the coat skirts were ordered to be sewn permanently up in the turned-back position illustrated, with the tips decorated sometimes with 'grenades' of cloth or brass; on campaign they were secured with hooks and eyes. This corporal also wears white linen knee-cuffs to protect his breeches from the stiff leather tops of his black cloth gaiters.

A3 Private, Battalion Company, 64th Foot

The 64th, later the Prince of Wales's North Staffordshire Regiment, wore black facings and regimental lace with one red and one black stripe in it; officers' metal was gold. The regiment fought throughout the war, taking part in the occupation of Boston and the fighting at Dorchester Heights, Long Island, Brandywine, Germantown and in the New Jersey and Southern campaigns.

Winter gaiters are shown here, long, with black bone buttons; summer pattern were mid-calf length only. The battalion companies – i.e. all the companies of a battalion except for the grenadier and light companies – were known as 'hat' companies; their cocked hat distinguished them from the special headgear of the élite companies. (These hats were often too small, and were kept in place by sewing two pieces of tape, as near as possible to the man's hair colour, to the lining of the hat, and fastening them with a hook and eye under the plait of hair at the back.) Linen had to be changed on Wednesdays and Sundays, and shoes were changed from foot to foot daily to prevent them 'running crooked'! On American service gaiter trousers or overalls were worn in the field, perhaps *over* the breeches and stockings. Records show that blue, brown and white cloth, striped ticking and old tents were all used to make these overalls.

The bayonet was carried in a frog on the waist-belt, but this was frequently worn over the right shoulder instead, leading eventually to the official issue of two crossbelts. From the left shoulder hung the cartridge-box, '. . . of stoutest blackened calfskin, with an inner flap of thick well painted linen. . . .' The box itself was a wooden block drilled with thirty-six holes, each for a paper cartridge.

For confirmation of other details, see 1768 Warrant quoted in text.

B1 Private, Battalion Company, 49th Foot, marching order

The 49th, later the Royal Berkshire Regiment, wore green facings, and lace in 'bastion' loops decorated with red and green lines. This soldier is shown in summer dress, with half-length gaiters. Note the pigtail of hair tucked up under the hat. The knapsack could be of painted canvas, as here, or of white goatskin. Haversacks were of greyish linen, and worn on the left hip, with a tin canteen. Note the large flap of the cartridge-box, to protect the other loads when the pouch was opened in wet weather. The hooked-back coat skirts are ornamented with the little brass hearts, since dug up in such numbers in America. The 'necessaries' for a soldier included: two white stocks, one black horsehair stock, brass clasps or buckles for these, three pairs of white yarn stockings, two pairs linen socks dipped in oil (to be worn on the march under spatterdashes – short gaiters), one pair long black gaiters with tops, one pair spatterdashes, one red forage cap, black leather garters, cleaning

materials, combs, brushes, rations, water, blanket, ammunition, and musket and bayonet. This musket has been immortalized as 'Brown Bess' – the weapon in service with the British infantry, with only minor changes, from well before the Seven Years War until well after the Napoleonic Wars. The flintlock land service musket, a ·75-calibre smooth-bore weapon weighing about ten pounds, without the socket bayonet, could, in the hands of steady and well-trained men under perfect conditions, deliver one shot every fifteen seconds or so.

B2 Drummer, 31st Foot, marching order

This drummer is dressed according to the Royal Warrant of 1768, for regiments with buff facings – i.e. the drummer wears red waistcoat and breeches and a coat of the facing colour. The 31st was later the East Surrey Regiment; regimental lace – which is used with a free hand to decorate the musicians' coats '. . . as the Colonel shall think fit . . .' – was white with blue, yellow and red stripes for the men, and silver for the officers. This man wears the white goatskin knapsack, on the normal harness which included a strap across the chest uniting the shoulder-straps. The bearskin cap had a similar plate to that of the grenadiers, but incorporating trophies of flags and drums in the motif.

Officially, the regiments had only drummers and fifers, and extra musicians for a band were unofficial and supported by the officers out of their own pockets. Often they were magnificently and fancifully uniformed; Negroes were popular in this capacity, and the flourishes of the modern drum major may have derived from the tricks and 'capers' performed by these men. The usual infantry band might consist of two each of bassoons, horns, clarionets, and possibly oboes; the trumpet might also have appeared. Although the bugle horn was introduced during the Revolutionary War, infantry regiments usually used the drum for signalling.

B3 Ensign, 55th Foot, with Regimental colour

The two colours, the King's and Regimental, of each infantry battalion, served as a rallying-point and a station-keeping device in battle, and like all standards throughout military history were an important psychological factor in the morale of the regiment. Their design is described in the Royal Warrant quoted in the body of the text. They were carried by ensigns, the junior commissioned rank; while in theory these officers might be of any age they were usually very young, sometimes only in their mid-teens. The officer illustrated wears the regulation uniform prescribed in the Warrant, with the green facings and gold lace of the 55th Foot, later to become the 2nd Battalion, the Border Regiment. His commissioned rank is indicated particularly by his gilt gorget, bearing the royal arms and regimental number and suspended from the coat collar buttons on a ribbon of facing colour; his sword, with gold and red sword-knot; and his crimson silk waist-sash. The colours, which must have been a considerable burden, were six feet by six feet six inches, on a pole nine feet ten inches high.

C1 Major-General in frock-coat

An order of 1767 prescribed two coats for British general officers. The uniform coat, richly laced with gold, was worn on state occasions. The scarlet 'frock' faced with blue was ornamented with gold-embroidered buttonholes, set in pairs for major-generals and threes for lieutenant-generals. There seems to have been no uniformity in the wearing of epaulettes – one or two, in gold, are believed to have been worn by both these ranks. The coat lining was buff until 1772, and white thereafter. A third style of coat, the 'undress frock' similar to the frock but lacking the gold buttonholes, was worn for some time before being officially sanctioned in 1786. A gold-laced cocked hat would have been worn, and a privately purchased sword.

Generals dressed, and lived, like the gentlemen they were, often taking enormous quantities of personal baggage and paraphernalia into the field, and reproducing as closely as possible the conditions of country-house life.

C2 Officer of Royal Artillery

The Royal Artillery already had a high reputation for professional skill, cleanliness, and imposing appearance; the largest and best-built recruits were picked for this service, which required a good deal of brutally hard work in handling guns.

From 1771 to 1775 the 4th Battalion replaced the R.A. units which had previously been serving in America; four companies of the 3rd Battalion later came out as reinforcements, and four companies drawn from the 1st and 3rd Battalions are known to have accompanied Burgoyne's army on its doomed march to Saratoga in 1777. These latter wore cut-down uniforms – as did the whole army – and altered their hats (see Plate G1), adding a red crest. The 4th Battalion are known to have worn a black feather in their hats, and an undress uniform of blue jacket and brown trousers.

This officer wears the blue uniform coat, faced with red and laced with gold, of his corps. He wears the usual crimson sash and a sword; the use of fusils and pouches by artillery officers was discontinued in about 1770. Officers and men wore white stocks, and the hair was clubbed when on duty.

C3 Gunner, Hesse-Cassel Field Artillery, 1776–82

More than thirty per cent of the British forces in North America were hired from the German states – a mercenary arrangement dignified by the close links between the British crown and various German royal houses. Hesse-Cassel provided the largest contingent, and also the best dressed and equipped. Because of their numbers, all German troops in America tended to be called 'Hessians' by British and colonists alike, but in fact units from Brunswick, Hesse-Hanau, Waldeck, Anspach-Bayreuth and Anhalt-Zerbst also served the British crown.

The entire artillery of Hesse-Cassel (three field companies, of which two had to be newly raised!) was contracted to Britain in January 1776, and spent until March training with their guns according to British methods. The first detachment landed on Staten Island in mid-August after a voyage from Bremen, and fought on Long Island about a week later. Thereafter, one or other element of this corps took part in nearly every important action of the war. Each company had an establishment of five officers, fourteen N.C.O.s, and 129 men. The guns are thought to have been four-pounders in the main, though other calibres were also used. Gun crews varied, but a typical crew might consist of a sergeant in command, a corporal gun-layer, two gunners (a vent tender and a firer), and from six to twelve other men –

matrosses – to help manœuvre the piece. The gunner illustrated here would not in fact use all the equipment he is carrying – a combined sponge and rammer, and a *bricole* for hauling the gun.

The uniform of the Hesse-Cassel artillery was not dissimilar to that of their British and continental contemporaries in that it consisted of a dark blue coat faced in red. However, in this case the red was more crimson than scarlet; the coat had no collar, and the smallclothes were of a yellowish shade. The black hat was laced white with a blue-over-red pompon and two similarly coloured tufts; all buttons were yellow metal, and a slung musket and side-arm were normal armament. This gunner has the large round artillery powder-flask, with brass trim, slung on a wide white belt complete with a vent-pricker on a chain. A waistbelt supports a small cartridge-box for musket ammunition. It has been stated elsewhere that bombardiers wore special caps with metal frontal plates, but this is now thought to be without foundation, at least as regards service in North America.

D1 Ensign with Regimental standard, Brunswick Infantry Regiment von Rhetz, 1776–7

A German regiment might be known by the name of its *chef*, its *kommandeur*, or its field commander. The *chef* was a colonel-in-chief, usually a member of the royal family or a prestigious general granted the title as an honour. The *kommandeur* was a senior officer, who might well not actually command the unit in the field, in which case it might be known by the name of the officer who did. Sometimes all three positions were held by one and the same man, but often not; and the constant changes in command, internal reorganizations (and differences of contemporary spelling) make it extremely difficult to identify some units.

This regiment was first raised in 1748, and received this designation in 1773; its *chef* was Major-General August von Rhetz. It was secured for American service by the British Government in 1776, and landed near Quebec on 27 September of that year. It took part in Burgoyne's 1777 campaign, after suffering a hard winter at Fort St Anne; after 'Gentleman Johnny's' 1st German Brigade disappeared into limbo with the rest of

his army, such small details of the 'von Rhetz' as had been left in Canada (sick, etc.) were incorporated into the Regiment von Ehrenkrook, and finished the war as garrison troops in the Trois Rivières area. The regiment's muster roll of October 1776 records one lieutenant-colonel, one major, five captains, five first- and five second-lieutenants, five ensigns; one each adjutant, quartermaster, chaplain, paymaster, surgeon-major, clerk and drum-major; five company surgeons, and four buglers; fifty sergeants and corporals, fifteen drummers, forty-one officers' valets, and 529 soldiers. (The Grenadier Company was on detached service at this time, but otherwise this may be taken as a fairly typical establishment.)

The Brunswick contingent was the second largest but the worst dressed and equipped among the German forces in America. When they arrived in Portsmouth *en route* for America the British Government had to spend £5,000 bringing their clothing up to standard – although even then they were cheated by rascally English contractors, receiving shipments of ladies' slippers instead of soldiers' shoes! The coarse cloth of the uniforms was of the cheapest type, the lapels could not be buttoned across, and in the absence of overcoats there were several deaths from cold. Once a proper system of supply was established the whole army received special winter clothing; long cloth overalls, woollen caps, mittens, under-jackets, and Canadian blanket coats. The summer overall trousers were often made of striped 'ticken' (see Plate D2).

The regimental uniform of the 'von Rhetz' was as illustrated here, although this ensign has certain rank distinctions. The hats of the men were bound with white and bore a red pompon and red tufts. The ensign is also distinguished by his cane, and his gold-lace trim at the cuffs. All ranks wore side-arms, and buttons spaced one-two-one down the lapels. The layout of the common soldier's personal equipment was very similar to that of the redcoat of the day, although a knapsack of brown fur was worn slung from the right shoulder and hanging behind the left arm, over the haversack, canteen and sword and bayonet frog. Soldiers also wore white shoulder-straps on the left shoulder, over the cartridge-box crossbelt.

Ojibway garters and moccasins dating from about 1780, collected by Colonel Arent De Peyster, commandant at Michilimackinac in 1774–9. Indian work of this type would have been adopted by British soldiers to some extent, depending on their distance from civilization and the type of duty they were performing. This attractive quill and bead decoration, with brass or copper 'tinkling cones' typical of frontier ornamentation of hair, clothes and equipment, must surely have caught the soldiers' eyes, if only as souvenirs. (Courtesy, City of Liverpool Museums)

D2 Grenadier, Hesse-Hanau Infantry Regiment Erbprinz, 1776

Another of the regiments which accompanied Burgoyne to Saratoga, the 'Erbprinz' provided its grenadier company for Lieutenant-Colonel Breymann's 'German Reserve' of grenadier and light companies. (This renowned tyrant was shot by his own men after he sabred four of his fleeing grenadiers on the field of Bennington.) The grenadier illustrated, who wears ticken overall trousers for summer field dress in place of the regulation white breeches and long black gaiters, is distinguished by his tall mitre cap; the fusiliers of the regiment are also thought to have worn a metal-fronted cap, but of lower profile. The white shoulder-knot or *aiguilette* seems to be the regimental distinction of the 'Erbprinz', worn on the right shoulder by all ranks. In action, a small black cartridge-box, decorated with the monogram of the Erbprinz Wilhelm of Hesse-Hanau, would be worn centrally on the front of the waistbelt. All types of troops in this unit are thought to have worn side-arms.

D3 Musketeer, Anhalt-Zerbst Infantry Regiment, 1781

This imposing figure, described by an eyewitness in New York in 1781, displays the Austrian influence which contrasts markedly with the Prussian-inspired uniforms of the other German contingents in America. The felt hussar-style cap was certainly replaced by a cocked hat in the field, and the breeches and top-boots by linen overalls. There is also evidence that the red waistcoat was replaced by a linen item. The white coat is faced with red on lapels, cuffs and shoulder-straps, and lined with the same colour. The coat buttons were yellow, those of the white-lined red waistcoat were of white. The red cloak and red-and-yellow sash would certainly have been discarded except when on formal duties.

The Anhalt-Zerbst contingent did not have an easy passage to America. The principality, which lay about twenty miles south-east of Magdeburg, had only some 20,000 inhabitants, from among whom their absentee ruler blithely promised Britain a regiment of two battalions of 550 men each. He had to recruit outside his own domains, and then had extraordinary difficulty getting his regiment to the sea. Frederick the Great of Prussia refused him passage through his territory, and an extremely devious route had to be taken to the coast, through seven other states. Desertions, and keen-eyed Prussian recruiting officers, reduced the force by about forty per cent *en route*. Some 600 men finally sailed in April 1778, to be followed by reinforcements in the three following years. The troops were used as garrisons in Canada and in New York until the end of hostilities, and never saw action.

E1 Corporal, Foot Jägers, Hesse-Cassel Field Jäger Corps

The German *jägers* were the élite marksmen of the British armies in America. The Hesse-Cassel *jägers* had fought against the French in Europe in 1758, and were recruited from the huntsmen, game-keepers and foresters of the principality. By the summer of 1777 there were five foot companies and one mounted squadron in America, officially assembled in a corps with an establishment of just over 1,000 men – although it is doubtful if actual strength was even half that, and the 'corps' was invariably broken up into small detachments. The *jägers* saw action in all the major campaigns of the war, but always in small units, in keeping with their role. The uniform consisted of green coats, waistcoats and breeches, the former faced and cuffed in crimson, with paired white metal buttons; the white lace illustrated here identifies corporal's rank. In summer white or buff linen breeches would not have been uncommon. (The green clothing associated with foresters of many nationalities since the earliest times – one thinks immediately of Robin Hood and his men clad in 'Lincoln green' – was the natural choice for *jäger* uniforms; in this specific connection it had been in use since 1744 by Prussian *jägers*, and has recurred again and again in the uniforms of rifle-men of many nations, up to the present day.) On parade green cockades and tall green feathers were added to the hats. The heavy, short-barrelled *jäger* rifles were very often personally owned weapons which the men had used in the woods of their homeland. The barrels, which were frequently octagonal, did not take bayonets, and the men

carried short hunting swords as side-arms, with traditional decorations at hilt and pommel, and decorated shell-guards. Ammunition was carried in a pouch slung on the waistbelt.

E2 Officer, Grenadier Company, 10th Foot

The 10th, later the Royal Lincolnshire Regiment, arrived in Boston from Canada in 1768 and was shipped back to Britain in 1778 after fighting at Lexington, Breed's Hill, Long Island, White Plains, Brandywine, Germantown and Monmouth Courthouse. This officer wears the regiment's bright yellow facings, and the silver lace of the 10th. Each regiment had its 'metal' colour – silver or gold – governing the colour of officers' epaulettes, sword-hilts, buttons, lace, gorgets and so forth. Officers of the grenadier companies wore two epaulettes, while battalion company officers wore one on the right only. Grenadier officers, like their men, wore bearskin caps; the cap, distinguished by a Roman regimental number on the crown, and the rest of the uniform illustrated, conforms to the 1768 Warrant quoted in the text. The sole exception is the wearing of tassels on the cap – unofficial, but common. Grenadier officers carried fusils and wore cartridge-boxes on cross-belts. An interesting item of trivia which survives is the note that in 1770 this regiment had a drummer and eight musicians; and that in 1778 £7 11s. 6d. was spent on painting the drums.

E3 Sergeant, Battalion Company, 29th Foot

Dressed according to the 1768 Warrant, this sergeant wears the plain white lace, and crimson sash with a stripe of facing colour, which identified his rank. He carries the halberd of his rank, though this would be exchanged for a musket when on campaign; it was used largely for ordering the ranks and giving signals during drill, and was too flimsy to serve as a weapon. (It is thought that some regiments whose 'metal' colour was gold may have had brass halberds.) The regimental distinctions of the 29th – later the Worcestershire Regiment – were yellow ochre facings, silver metal for officers, and white lace with two blue and one yellow stripes for corporals, privates and musicians. (The 29th had, in 1774, ten Negro drummers.) The gaiter buttons of grenadiers were of white metal instead of the usual black bone or horn.

In winter no overcoats were issued, although thirty caped 'watch coats' per regiment were kept for the use of sentries in cold weather. The sentry on duty in Boston on 5 March 1770 probably wore one. He was pelted with snowballs by a large and threatening mob of Bostonians, and the guard, consisting of an officer and eight men, was called out. The rabble continued to harass them, and in the confusion shots were fired. Five 'patriots' died; thanks to their American lawyer, all except two of the soldiers were acquitted at the subsequent trial, and the two were – rightly – not punished severely for their part in the so-called 'Boston Massacre'.

F1 Private, 17th Light Dragoons, on service with Tarleton's British Legion
This regiment, later the 17th/21st Lancers, was raised by the officer who brought the King news of Wolfe's victory and death at Quebec, and its death's-head badge – still in use today – commemorates that victory and death, as did the black line in the regimental lace. At various times the skull of the crested helmet was brass, at other times black. The 1768 Warrant describes the coats of the regiment as red with white facings, white metal buttons in pairs, and white linings. Smallclothes were also white. Officers' silver lace had a black edge at the buttonholes, and officers at an inspection in 1771 '. . . carry their cloaks of Mazarine blue, lined with white. . . .' (Mazarine blue was a deep, rich blue shade.)

The 17th left Ireland for America in 1775, and landed in Boston just before Bunker (Breed's) Hill. A small detachment took part in the fight, and detachments served in most of the important engagements throughout the war. Short cloth gaiters were worn for dismounted service. This dragoon, on service with Tarleton's famous Provincial cavalry, has – like his comrades – preferred to keep and patch his regimental jacket instead of accepting the dress of the Legion; although worn-out breeches and boots have been replaced by gaiter trousers and shoes, and the red silk turban on his helmet by sheepskin. During hot weather in the southern campaigns the men wore white linen 'frocks' or smocks in the field.

Equipment recorded as shipped for American service included four rifled carbines per troop, corn sacks, nosebags, haversacks with leather straps, water-bottles, felling axes, iron kettles with bags, hatchets, bell tents, camp colours and 192 billhooks for dismounted men. The normal armament of the trooper was the heavy straight sword and a pair of pistols.

F2 Officer, 16th (Queen's) Light Dragoons, 1776–8
The second of the two British cavalry regiments which served in America was the 16th Light Dragoons. General Sir John Burgoyne was their colonel in 1766, when they wore black facings; blue came with the change of title to 'Queen's' late in that year, as all Royal regiments wore blue facings. The men had white lace, the officers and sergeants, silver; corporals had a narrow silver edge round the top of the blue coat cuff. Sergeants were further distinguished by the usual waist-sash with a central stripe of the blue facing colour. The white metal buttons were set in pairs; the smallclothes were white. The black helmet had a blue turban, and a red plume rising from a crest with brass trim. The frontal device was in white. The sash was knotted on the right hip, as with all mounted regiments. The design of the black and silver officers' epaulettes illustrated here is copied from contemporary portraits.

The 16th transferred its effective horses and men to the 17th Light Dragoons and returned home after the British retreat from Philadelphia in 1778. No doubt these troopers continued to wear their blue-faced coats, at least until they wore out and could not be replaced. A light infantry or dismounted troop was added to the regiment for service in America. They wore leather helmets like the light infantry, brown cloth gaiters instead of boots, and carried cloaks and hatchets. No broadswords were carried.

F3 Private, Brunswick Dragoon Regiment Prinz Ludwig Ernst, 1776–7
Raised in 1698, this regiment was designated a dragoon unit in 1772. Its *kommandeur* was Major-General Freidrich Riedesel, commander of the entire Brunswick contingent, so it was commanded in the field by Lieutenant-Colonel Friedrich Baum,

who was mortally wounded at Bennington. The regiment reached Quebec on 1 June 1776; it mustered twenty officers and 316 men organized into four troops each of three officers and seventy-five men, with a staff of eight officers and sixteen men. Although completely equipped for mounted service, the regiment sailed without horses and was expected to mount itself on arrival in America. In fact it was never mounted, and served on foot with Burgoyne's army, wearing gaiters instead of the heavy boots usual for mounted service. (This would hardly have been an insurmountable hardship for dragoons, whose function has been that of 'mounted infantry' since the seventeenth century.) They fought with great courage, and nearly all were killed or captured at Bennington.

Officers wore a silver *aiguilette* on the right shoulder, silver lace on their uniforms, silver sword-knots and a silver-and-black sash. All ranks wore white plumes for parade occasions. The drummers were Negroes, and wore reversed colours – yellow lined and faced with light blue. The drum major must have looked extremely splendid in this uniform, heavily trimmed with silver lace.

G1 Private, 62nd Foot, 1777
In 1775 the 62nd Foot – later the Wiltshire Regiment – were inspected at Cork, Ireland, and the inspecting general observed 'uniforms very short and hats very small . . . coats cut so short that I must call them jackets. Hats too small. Poor Regiment.' (It is pleasant to record that the inspection report of 1787 calls them a 'smart, pretty regiment'.) It seems that the 62nd were anticipating the orders issued to Burgoyne's army in 1777, and earned that time-hallowed military rebuke, 'Wait for it!' All the regiments under Burgoyne's command, including the artillery, were to reduce their coats to jackets and their cocked hats to caps, so that the whole force would look like light infantry. Roaches of fur and hair, dyed in different colours, were fixed to the caps. The pocket flaps on this figure, which is based on a contemporary sketch, are vertical instead of horizontal as was more usual. They were false pockets, and it may have been thought that they looked 'prettier' this way. The facings of the 62nd were pale yellowish buff, and as with all regiments

with buff facings, the smallclothes are of the same colour. The device on the front of the cap is unclear. The 20th, 21st, 24th and 47th Foot all wore similarly cropped uniforms.

G2 Light Infantryman, Battle of Germantown, 1777
It is highly probable that British uniforms were adapted to campaign conditions to a far greater extent than we usually accept. The only contemporary drawings show much-altered clothing, and this is backed up by letters, diaries and the descriptions of deserters circulated at the time. Hats were cropped, or 'uncocked' and worn in the popular round form. This uniform is based on a painting of the Battle of Germantown, reputedly prepared from the description of an officer who was present. The light infantryman wears a short jacket or sleeved waistcoat without facings or lace, and linen gaiter trousers. His hat is decorated with an animal tail, and his crossbelt is black.

G3 Officer, 5th Foot, 1777
This officer of the 5th – later the Northumberland Fusiliers – is partly based on the same painting of Germantown. His 'regimentals' are faced 'gosling green' and laced silver. His uncocked or round hat is decorated with a cockade and feathers. His hair is dressed according to contemporary fashion, and would have been powdered for parade. He wears the popular jockey boots and spurs. Officers' swords were supposed to be of a regimental pattern, chosen by the colonel, and of the regimental 'metal' colour, according to the Royal Warrant. In practice many officers seem to have pleased themselves, and curved swords with half-basket hilts were popular weapons.

All fusilier regiments were supposed to wear smaller versions of the black bearskin grenadier cap (see 1768 Warrant quotation), but a variety of caps of different patterns appear in contemporary sources. Some were peaked, and had transverse fur roaches; the 23rd (Royal Welch) seem to have worn hats with feathers placed to represent the Prince of Wales's feathers. Whether or not these styles were worn only by light companies, or by the whole battalion to save wear and tear on the expensive fur caps, is unconfirmed, but the latter explanation is not unlikely.

H1 Officer, 42nd Royal Highland Regiment, 1776
The Black Watch distinguished themselves in the French and Indian War, and returned to America in May 1776. They served throughout the War of Independence, and then moved to Halifax, Nova Scotia, in 1783 before returning to England in 1784.

This officer, based on a contemporary portrait, wears a uniform conforming to the 1768 Regulations; the coat is faced with dark blue and laced gold, with a white lining and waistcoat. The kilted plaid of 'government sett', the crimson sash worn across the left shoulder, and the stiffened Kilmarnock bonnet are the most obvious distinctions of the Highland officers. The latter has a diced band and a red tuft or 'touri' on top, and is decorated with black ostrich feathers. (These became thicker, taller and more numerous on the bonnets of officers and men alike as the years passed, eventually developing into the feathered head-dress still worn with musicians' ceremonial dress.) He carries the Highland broadsword, and a dirk, sporran and all-steel Scottish pistol.

H2 Private, 42nd Royal Highland Regiment, 1783
An inspection return filed after the regiment arrived in Nova Scotia stated that '. . . the 42nd could not appear in their full uniform for want of plaids, etc., which the C.O. thought proper annually to dispose of during the late War, to purchase a more commodious dress for the American service, with the approbation of the Commander-in-Chief. The regiment appeared remarkably clean dressed – the men had on white strong ticken trousers with short, black cloth gaiters.' It has not been established whether this abandoning of the plaid was due to shortages and supply difficulties, or to a desire for a more practical campaigning dress. At any event, this private is shown as he would have appeared on campaign, with overall trousers and no gaiters, but retaining his bonnet and short Highland jacket faced blue, and with the 42nd's bastion-shaped loops with a single red line in the lace. Leather equipment was black; it seems that a cartridge-box worn centrally at the waist began to give way to the conventional pattern in about 1780. Contemporary reports speak of the shortages of broadswords, and their unpopularity among the men in combat – most apparently preferred the bayonet, and even the grenadiers appeared on parade without swords. This soldier uses the frog to carry a cased hatchet.

H3 Officer, Flank Company, 42nd Royal Highland Regiment, 1783
Based on a contemporary portrait, this figure illustrates the appearance of an officer in the field, after the regiment had given up the kilt for trousers. His breeches are worn with ordinary black infantry gaiters with leather tops. He retains the sash and gorget of rank, and his broadsword, but carries a soldier's canteen and a cartridge-box on his waist-belt with loads for his fusil, or light musket. These were usually carried by officers of the flank – grenadier or light – companies, and sometimes in the field by battalion company officers as well. On parade the latter carried espontoons, light steel-headed half-pikes about seven feet long with a small cross-bar below the blade. These were useful for making a graceful salute and signalling evolutions, but hardly practical as weapons under American conditions. Battalion officers wore a single epaulette, usually an unstiffened strap of gold or silver lace with a fringe; flank company officers wore two epaulettes, or the lace shoulder-ornaments – 'wings' – illustrated here.

Frazer's Highlanders were re-raised during the war as the 71st, and wore a uniform similar to the 42nd, with the 'government sett' plaid, but with white jacket facings.